The Finale Primer

Mastering the Art of Music Notation
with Finale

by Bill Purse

Chair, Music Technology Department

Duquesne University

For Finale 2000 and Above

*For Both Windows & Macintosh
Computer Platforms*

**Miller
Freeman
Books**

San Francisco

Published by Miller Freeman Books
600 Harrison Street, San Francisco, CA 94107
Publishers of *Keyboard*, *Bass Player*, and *Guitar Player* magazines

 Miller Freeman
A United News & Media publication

Distributed to the book trade in the U.S. and Canada by
Publishers Group West, 1700 Fourth Street, Berkeley, CA 94710

Distributed to the music trade in the U.S. and Canada by
Hal Leonard Publishing, P.O. Box 13819, Milwaukee, WI 53213

Design and Typesetting: Greene Design

Library of Congress Cataloging-in-Publication Data:
Purse, Bill.
 The Finale primer: mastering the art of music notation with
 Finale: for Finale 2000 and above: for both Windows &
 Macintosh computer platforms / by Bill Purse — 2nd ed.
  p. cm.
 Includes index.
 ISBN 0-87930-602-5 (alk. paper)
 1. Finale (Computer file) 2. Music notation — Data processing
 I. Title.
MT39.P88 2000
780'. 1'4802855369—dc21   00-020239

Printed in the United States of America
00 01 02 03 5 4 3 2 1

Table of Contents

Preface

During my precomputer days spent mastering the exacting art of music notation, I often daydreamed of an electronic scribe who could generate engraved music via the push of a button! In 1988, Coda realized my fantasy with its introduction of Finale, a state-of-the-art notation program for computer users. Finale combined sophisticated real-time MIDI implementation with comprehensive notational graphic options. These options include: music transcription as you play, immediate playback on a MIDI instrument with your timbre of choice, MIDI-controlled realization of dynamics and expression markings, fluid lyric insertion and alignment, and creation of custom guitar grids. Finale's flexible computer realization of simple to complex notation is a blessing for composers, orchestrators, arrangers, copyists, and music publishers. In fact, Coda's Finale truly is this electronic scribe, capable of addressing any imaginable type of twenty-first-century notation task.

Acknowledgments

My special thanks go to my wife and late-night editor, Lynn Purse. Additional thanks to Dr. Judith Bowman; Ken Karsh; Duquesne University's School of Music students; Duquesne University's Summer Session graduate students; Professor Emeritus Matty Shiner (the reason this book exists); Mark Koch; Jay Weaver; Joe Negri; Don Muro; David Mash at Berklee; Tom Johnson, Kathleen Fanelli, and David Pogue at Coda; Lee Whitmore, Mike Kovins, and Mike Lamb at SoundTree; Paul Youngblood at Roland USA; Dr. Tom Rudolph, John Dunphy, and George Pinchot at Villanova/TI:ME; Bill Schultz, Ed Rizzuto, and Bob Shomaker at Fender Musical Instruments; Big Bill Purse; Wolf Marshall at Hal Leonard Pub.; Greg Irwin; Michael Bates at Yamaha USA; Leroy Esau at Kurzweil; Andrew Knox; Bill Bay at Mel Bay Publications; Scott Wilkinson at *Electronic Musician,* Jon Chappel at *Guitar* magazine; Herb Deutsch at Hofstra University; Will Schmit; Chuck Caplan.

The author would also like to thank the following for their considerable support: Joy Carden, Larry Morton at Hal Leonard Publishing, Larry Harms at Roland USA.

The author is deeply grateful for the advice and assistance of the editors and staff at Miller Freeman: Matt Kelsey, Dorothy Cox, Jan Hughes, Nancy Tabor and Corinna Cornejo; copy editor Carolyn Keating; proofreader Roger Mensink; and designer Brad Greene.

About the Author

Bill Purse is Chair of the Music Technology and Guitar Departments at Duquesne University, where he was instrumental in the development of two new majors: Music Technology and Sound Recording Technology. Purse is the past chair of the MENC/NAMM/GAMA Guitar Task Force, which was created to revitalize the guitar in education. This very successful task force has retrained over 525 teachers, who in turn have taught over 120,000 new guitarists. Purse is also the editor of the MENC publication *Strategies for Teaching Guitar in Middle and High School*. He is also a member of the Advisory Board for TI:ME (Technology Institute for Music Educators), as well as a certified teacher of TI:ME workshops. Bill can be reached by email at: MaestroBP@AOL.COM.

Purse received his B.M. and M.M. at Duquesne University, and an EDUCOM grant for study with Dr. Carol Lennox at Mills College in the area of multimedia development in 1990. In addition, Purse has studied privately with Howard Massey at the Center for Electronic Music in New York, and with Pat Martino. As the author of *Bach Chorales for Guitar* (Mel Bay Publications) and *The Duquesne University Guitar Method* (Lyrrus/G-Vox), Purse has pioneered the utilization of interactive CD-ROMs, MIDI files, hard disk recording, and music score publication in classroom environments. Purse has integrated music technology software into all areas of his classroom and private teaching at Duquesne University. He has specialized in developing accelerated courses for mastering the guitar, *The Guitar Atlas* and *Basic Guitar Structures*, and has also written a book for the new Warner Bros. Ultimate Beginner Tech Start Series™: *Home Recording Basics*.

Purse has performed in concert with Al DiMeola, Turtle Island String Quartet, Emily Remler, Joe Pass, Leni Stern, Barney Kessel, Herb Ellis, Larry Carlton, Billy Cobham, Al Martino, Lou Christie and The Butler Symphony, and has been a featured artist at arts festivals, including the Three Rivers Arts Festival, Shadyside Jazz Festival, Mellon Jazz Festival, Music Teachers National Association (Dallas, TX), Music Educators National Association (Kansas City, KS), and the International Association of Jazz Educators (Anaheim, CA/Chicago, IL). Purse has also performed as the pit guitarist for the stage productions of *Fame* and *Godspell* with the Civic Light Orchestra at the Benedum Theater in Pittsburgh, and *Tommy* for Gargaro Productions at the Byham Theater in Pittsburgh.

As a consultant for Fender Musical Instruments and Apple Computer, Purse is a frequent and well-known lecturer and clinician on guitar synthesis and computer/MIDI applications for the guitar. Purse was a staff writer for *MIDI Guitarist* and *Electronic Musician*, and has been featured in articles published in the *Roland Users Guide*, *Korg Pro-View*, and *Guitar Player* magazine.

A composer, arranger, and producer in radio and television, Purse has produced and released several albums of original music, including Catch 22's *Reappearance* and Aergo's *Free*. He has toured worldwide with the synthesizer ensemble Aergo, and is the producer, arrranger, and guitarist for the Duquesne faculty guitar ensemble Catch 22.

Introduction

The elaborate rules established for modern notational practice require a computer notation program that not only addresses these rules but also performs in a sophisticated, intuitive manner. Finale fills this need by translating musical rules such as durations, formatting and beaming automatically, with user override capability. Finale understands notes as data representations of pitches to be transposed and edited at will. Finale's intuitive understanding of the rules of music notation can be an asset for users with limited musical knowledge. For many notational challenges, Finale remains the solution. Today, Finale has grown to be the world's number one notation software and the second most popular general music software.

The Finale Primer is a cross platform book that works with both Macintosh and Windows computer platforms. Windows Finale uses Windows 95/98/NT as its interface; the main differences from the Macintosh version are the keyboard shortcuts and window displays.

In instances where the Windows and Mac platforms diverge, separate instructions are given for each. Special icons Mac ⌘-1 and Windows Ctrl/+/ will appear in the text to call attention to information specific to each of these platforms. Your computer's speed and power, regardless of which computer platform you work with, determine the speed of Finale in drawing, printing, and executing commands. Keep in mind that when the book shows a keyboard shortcut using the Command key on the Mac, you will use the Control key in Windows. Appendix 8 will show you a direct comparison between Windows and Macintosh keyboard shortcuts. If you have friends or colleagues who do not use Macintosh or Windows, you can exchange files with them using Finale's ETF (see Appendix 1, "Finale and Computer Terminology") format.

Once you are comfortable with Finale's interface, the benefits in speed and high quality output make it time to put away the pen and pencil. *The Finale Primer* will help you with music preparation, whether copying an existing piece of music or creating an original work. You will find Finale invaluable in editing, reformatting, and reorganizing musical material, and *The Finale Primer* a solid first step in understanding and utilizing this powerful program.

The Finale Primer's organization of information is similar to the way a notator normally works to create handwritten scores. It presents the necessary Finale navigational skills up front and reinforces notational concepts by providing drills and projects at the end of each chapter. My experience in teaching music technology at Duquesne University's Music School for more than fourteen years has dramatically pointed out the need for an individual or classroom Finale text. *The Finale Primer* provides short, concise drills that do not replace manuals but greatly shorten Finale's robust learning curve.

The purpose of *The Finale Primer* is not to replace the online manuals but to help you make better use of them when you run into a tricky notational challenge. *The Finale Primer* also includes appendices that explore specific notational topics in more depth. It is advisable to purchase a text on music notation to help you understand the finer points of music scoring (see Bibliography).

You should always have your on-line manuals handy as in-depth references, but due to the size of the manuals and the massive information required to master Finale, *The Finale Primer* is your first step and guide toward expert user status.

Computer Notation and the
National Standards for the Arts

In January 1994, the Goals 2000: Educate America Act, specified the arts as
essential elements within the core curriculum for American students. As a
result, the National Committee for Standards in the Arts announced this
country's first *voluntary* arts standards. This publication, *National Standards
for Arts Education*, resulted from a national consensus among artists, professional education associations, teachers, parents, and leaders in all areas of
the arts. It focused on what kindergarten to 12th grade students should
know and be able to do in the arts as a direct result of their instruction.

A direct offshoot of this publication was one published by a MENC
(Music Teacher National Conference) Task Force entitled *The School Music
Program; A New Vision* (see Bibliography), which isolates music from the
dance and theater areas in the original document. The following nine
content standards for music listed below provide a guide for improving
music curriculum and present a balanced comprehensive approach in
curriculum sequencing and design.

Content Standards for Music

1. Singing, alone and with others, a varied repertoire of music.

2. Performing on instruments, alone and with others, a varied repertoire
   of music.

3. Improvising melodies, harmonies, and accompaniments.

4. Composing and arranging music within specified guidelines.

5. Reading and notating music.

6. Listening to, analyzing, and describing music.

7. Evaluating music and music performances.

8. Understanding relationships between music, the other arts, and
   disciplines outside the arts.

9. Understanding music in relation to history and culture.

One of the main tenets of the standards, referred to by the MENC administration, places a high priority on the use of technology in all nine areas. Incorporating a powerful notation program such as Finale into the music education environment can serve multiple standards in using technology to effectively teach music. It is important that all educators gain an understanding of the standards and reflect on their incorporation into the music classroom. A comprehensive book addressing the National Music Standards and the use of technology in music education is currently available by Dr. Tom Rudolph entitled *Teaching Music with Technology* (see Bibliography).

The following how-to topics are explored in depth in Dr. Rudolph's book and give you an idea of computer notation usage in music education:

- Create written presentations such as workbooks, method books, lead sheets, musical handouts, warm-up exercises, transposed parts, etc.

- Enhance personal composing and arranging skills.

- Experiment with orchestrations via MIDI playback.

- Introduce composition skills to your students through the creation of simple melodies with notation software.

- Expand your students' understanding of musical concepts—rhythm, melody and harmony—while receiving homework assignments with a professional appearance.

- Aid students in developing listening skills.

I find the nine content standards to be an invaluable evaluation tool for students' musical skills and comprehension within the music technology curriculum at Duquesne University. It is my sincere desire that music educators use the skills learned in *The Finale Primer* to help them create professional music materials, not only for themselves, but also for their students' exploration of the musical and computer skills Finale brings to the classroom.

Getting Started: Finale Basics

It is extremely important to take the time to understand program navigation and basics prior to music input to make your Finale technique as efficient as possible. Chapter One presents the necessary basic Finale skills;
completing the drills and projects in this and the following chapters will
aid in reinforcement. Bear in mind that *The Finale Primer* can function as
an individual or classroom text, providing concise information that short-
ens the program's learning curve.

Launching Finale*

Finale 2000

- Locate the folder called Finale 2000, and double-click its icon.

- Double-click the application icon Finale 2000 to launch or start
  the program.

- There are minor interface "look and feel" differences between the Mac and
  Windows versions, but when fully launched your screen will look something
  like this.

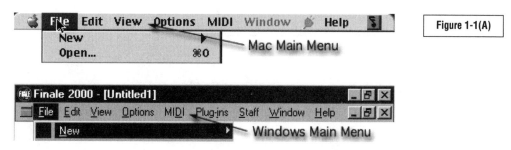

Figure 1-1(A)

---

* Installation of Finale software is covered in the program manual *Before You Begin*,
p. ix, and is not in the scope of this book.

- To create a new document you must click on the word **File** in the top menu bar and hold down the mouse button.

- Drag the pointer down until you get to the word **New**, then release the mouse button (see Figure 1-1[B]).

Figure 1-1(B)

Document With Setup Wizard...   Ctrl+N
Default Document

Document From Template...
Empty Document

- Notice that there is virtually no difference between the order of the commands for the Mac and Windows in Figure 1-1(A).

- Select Document With Setup Wizard. A Wizard is designed to help you set up your Finale document. Many other programs offer setup Wizards, such as Microsoft Office. Be careful of selecting **Empty Document** unless this is want you want, as styles and many other Finale features are not immediately available with this option. If you want to completely start a Finale document from scratch, use Empty Document. The Empty Document command will not be used in the *Finale Primer*.

- ⌘-N/Ctrl+N

- The setup dialog box appears in Figure 1-1 (C). Here you provide the Title and Composer:

- You also have the option to select a Finale document's orientation (portrait and landscape) and page size. Make sure that the Page setup for the

Figure 1-1(C)

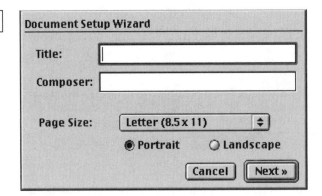

Document Setup Wizard

Title:

Composer:

Page Size: Letter (8.5 x 11)   ⬍

⦿ Portrait   ◯ Landscape

Cancel   Next »

printer is the same
orientation or
your output will
not be correct.
More on this topic
in Chapter Six.

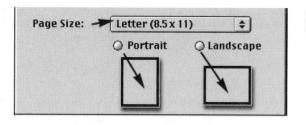

Figure 1-1(D)

• Select the **Next** Button

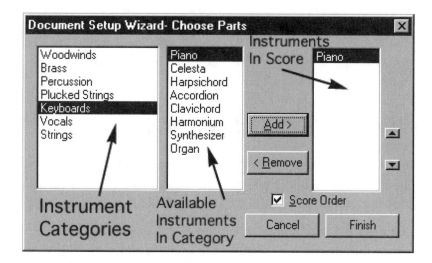

Figure 1-1(E)

• The dialog box in Figure 1-1 (E) appears offering three columns:

Instrument Categories

Specific Instruments (In the Selected Category)

Instruments In Score (An empty column that will contain a list of the instruments selected for the score).

The order that the instruments appear in the third column will be how they are displayed in the score.

If the Score Order Box is checked, Finale will automatically place instruments in the order that a traditional orchestral score would use.

Another option with the New command is Default Document, this is the one we will use for the drills in the following chapters. Notice that there is no shortcut for this command.

Figure 1-1(F)

When a window opens, it contains blank measures of music, usually in the treble clef, and is called the **default window** (see Appendix 1, "Finale and Computer Terminology"). This window displays a document's starting point and does not generally contain music notation.

The default window can be user-definable, allowing you to define a starting point for creating your score, e.g., a grand staff if you work with piano music, guitar and tablature systems if you work primarily with guitar transcriptions, etc. (See Appendix 3, "Creating a New Finale Default File" if you wish to create a new default window.)

Building Finale Navigational Skills

Study and become familiar with the components and descriptions of the generic Finale window in Figure 1-2(A). Across the top of the screen is a standard Macintosh/IBM pull-down **menu bar**. The right side of the screen has a vertical **scroll bar**, to move the view of the music up or down. Across the bottom of the screen is a horizontal scroll bar, to move left or right through the measures of your piece. The **measure counter** and its internal number specifies the leftmost visible measure.

To jump to any measure in the score, double-click the number in the measure counter field, type a new measure number into this field, and either press the **Return** key or the **Enter** key on your **alphanumeric keyboard** (see Figure 1-2[B]). (See Appendix 1, "Finale and Computer Terminology," for a definition of alphanumeric and an explanation of additional window components, e.g., Size box.)

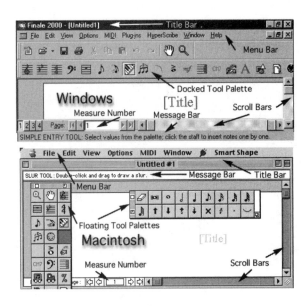

Figure 1-2(A)

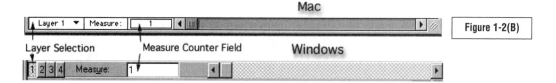

Mac

Figure 1-2(B)

Layer Selection Measure Counter Field Windows

Opening an Existing Document

- Locate the folder called Finale 2000 and double-click its icon. Double-click or select the application icon Finale 2000 to launch or start the program.

- Click on the word **File** in the top menu bar and hold down the mouse button. Drag the pointer down until you get to the word **Open**, then release the mouse button. A dialog box will appear that will allow you to search for the document on the hard drive or a floppy disk.

Finale Power Tools and Shortcuts

With Finale there are several ways to execute notation commands. The following sidebar presents information on **power keys**, the quickest way to perform a task with Finale.

Learn power keys—keyboard shortcuts that are the most efficient way to maneuver and complete a Finale task immediately. This will save you considerable time. Power key combinations allow you to use specific keyboard combinations as opposed to the mouse (selecting a command from the pull-down main menu) to perform a notation procedure. Power key utilization can save time in working with Finale and make you a power user. When a power key choice is available in Finale, *The Finale Primer* will encourage you to use it right from the start.

Special Finale insights will be presented in the margins with a gray triangle background.

The Power Key Icon

When you see the icon **P**, the following information will present a new keyboard shortcut. For multiple power key stroke sequences, press the left key in the text first, then the following key or keys, e.g., the Command key and then the letter N: ⌘-**N**/Ctrl+N. Windows shortcuts follow the forward slash.

Make sure that power keys become an important part of your Finale technique.

Figure 1-3 shows the location on the alphanumeric keyboard of power keys. Study Figure 1-3(A) and (B) to be aware of their location when specified in *The Finale Primer*. Since not all keyboards have certain keys in the same place, examine your keyboard for any differences.

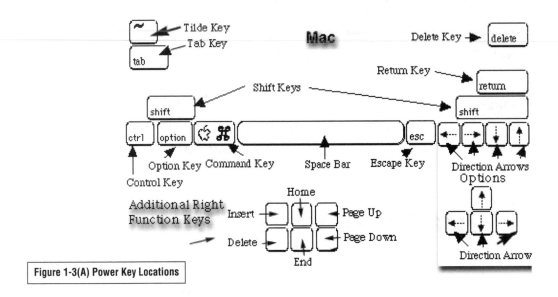

Figure 1-3(A) Power Key Locations

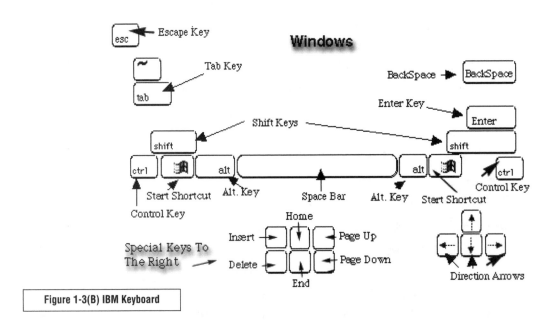

Figure 1-3(B) IBM Keyboard

The **Escape key** cancels a window.

The **Command** or **Apple key** Control or Ctrl is one of the most important power keys and will execute many Finale shortcuts when coupled with other keys.

The **Return key** right mouse click is the power key that triggers the OK button in a dialog box.

The **Option key** helps to expand the scope of the alphanumeric keyboard by providing special functions with the different tools.

The **Tab key** will allow you to move from field to field in a **dialog box** without clicking into another field with the mouse.

If a **handle** is selected for a number or word in a field, the **Delete/Backspace key** will eliminate it from your score.

When you are inputting notes, holding down the **Shift key/Shift and Number (1-8) above QWERTY only** will allow you to input rests.

The **direction arrows** nudge any selected handle for a staff, articulation, text, etc., in the direction of the key you press. This allows for very accurate positioning.

The **Control key/not available in Windows** is used to select staff sets, which you program, or to switch to tools that have been programmed.

(See Appendix 1, "Finale and Computer Terminology" for definitions and explanations of terms in *The Finale Primer*.)

The Message Bar

The **message bar** at the top of the document window Mac/Status bar at the bottom of the screen in Windows displays the name of each selected tool and provides a brief definition of how to use the selected tool (see Figure 1-4). It also displays status information during Finale operations. It can be hidden to take up less screen space (select **View** from the main Finale menu and select the **Hide Message Bar** command).

It is important to have the message bar available when you are beginning to use Finale as a convenient easy-to-see guide.

Figure 1-4

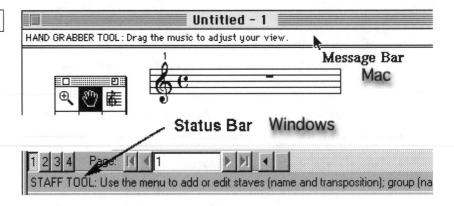

• If the message bar is not on the screen, select View from the main Finale menu and select the **Show Message Bar** command/Select Status Bar from Window in the main Finale menu.

To use power keys to hide or show the message bar, just press and hold the Command key and then the letter M: ⌘-**M**/Not available in Windows. It is usually easy to remember a power key shortcut, since the letter will frequently be the same as the first letter of the command word.

Help—Balloon Help and the Built-in Manual

Balloon Help provides Finale with a "screen-sensitive" help guide for general Macintosh functions. This built-in Mac help is available by simply choosing **Show Balloons** from the Help menu at the right end of the menu bar (see Figure 1-5). Move the cursor to any menu command, dialog box, etc., and a heading appears to explain the item selected. (A Finale help document is included with the software installation disks and must be loaded into your computer to have the Finale Balloon Help available in your Finale folder.)

• Click on **Help** in the main menu. Choose **Show Balloons**/Not available in Windows. Then point to items on the screen to see their Help balloons.

• To turn Balloon Help off, go to the main menu bar and select Hide Balloons.

When you install Finale, an additional program, Adobe Acrobat Reader 4.0, will be loaded into your computer. With this program installed, you

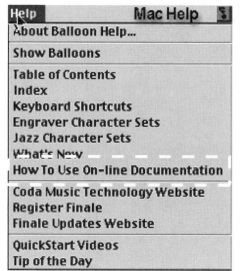
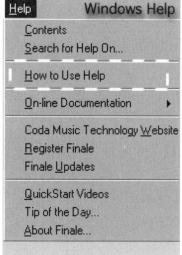

Figure 1-5

can use the On-line Documentation, a built-in manual. For more information on how to use On-line Documentation, select the menu item **How To Use On-line Help Documentation**.

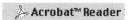

A Look at the Main Tool Palette

Figure 1-6 shows the **Main Tool Palette**. Placement and size are reconfigurable by the user for creating an efficient work area. The user can operate 28 selectable tools for the Mac/26 (Hand Grabber and Zoom In Main Tool Bar) for Windows. Each tool is devoted to a specific task, such as the input or editing of musical or graphic data, MIDI, lyrics, and page formatting. A tool is activated for a particular task by clicking on its icon. Some tools also bring up associated menus at the far right of the top main menu bar. When you select a certain tool, screen options that are editable acquire small handles and become selectable or moveable. Click on these handles or other editable elements in the main menu or a dialog box to edit or move them.

Figure 1-6

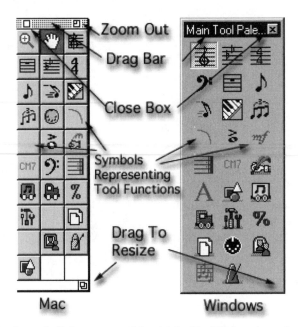

Zoom Out

Drag Bar

Close Box

Symbols Representing Tool Functions

Drag To Resize

Mac   Windows

- Open Finale and click on any of the Main Tool Palette's tools and notice how the information in the message bar/status bar changes to reflect the name of the tool selected and a brief description of how to use the selected tool.

The Main Tool Palette is almost always on the screen. If you cannot find it, simply open it by going to the **Window** menu in Finale and selecting the Main Tool Palette command.

Every time you use pull-down menus in Finale they will contain a special power key prompt to the right of the written command (see Figure 1-7 [A]). Every time you see one of these prompts is a good reminder to use power key options rather than the mouse. This power key prompt is not available in Windows for this particular option, but many other Windows commands have a prompt.

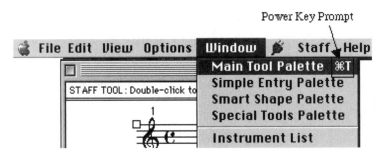

Figure 1-7(A)

14   THE FINALE PRIMER

To select the Main Tool Palette, press and hold the Command key and the letter T: ⌘-T/Not available in Windows.

The **Close box** in the upper left-hand corner of the palette will close the Main Tool Palette and remove it from the window (see Figure 1-7 [B]).

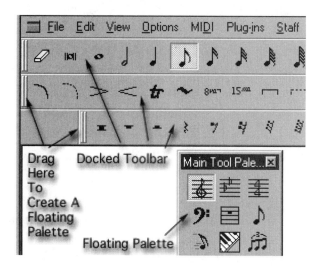

Figure 1-7(B)

The Windows version of Finale allows you to **dock** a tool palette as a **tool bar** that runs vertically below the main menu or to the left of the screen. To create a floating palette from a toolbar, click on the edge of the toolbar that has a slightly raised ridge and drag its outline to the center of the screen. (see Figure 1-7 [B]). Once this is accomplished you can drag and move the floating palette to any desired location on the screen.

To restore a floating palette to a docked toolbar, click the raised edge of the floating palette back to its original or new docked position and release it.

With both the Mac and Windows version of Finale you can hide or display tool palettes/toolbars for more space to see and work on your score. To accomplish this task simply select the tool palette or toolbar's name from the Window command in the main menu. Selecting the tool's name toggles a check mark on (display tool) or off (hide tool).

Reconfiguring the Main Tool Palette

When you resize the Main Tool Palette via the **Resize box** (Mac only), a dotted rectangle will appear to show you the new shape of the Main Tool Palette when the mouse is released. When you resize the Main Tool Palette in Windows, any contact with the cursor to an edge of the palette will bring up adjustment arrows.

If the reconfiguration is too small to allow access to all the tools, the **Zoom box** can be used to access all the tools in the palette.

Clicking anywhere in the **drag bar** and **dragging** produces a dotted outline of the Main Tool Palette to indicate its new location when the mouse is released.

By dragging the Resize Box diagonally upward and to the right, the entire palette can be reshaped.

Some Finale users like to reconfigure the Main Tool Palette horizontally, as in Figure 1-8 (B), and place it directly under the staff for inputting data.

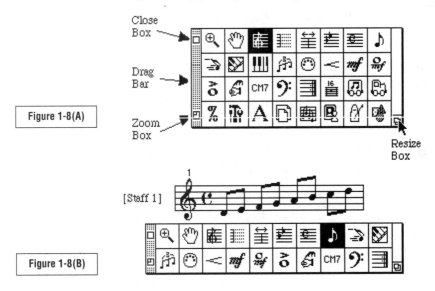

Figure 1-8(A)

Figure 1-8(B)

Selecting Tools from the Palette

- Select the **Mass Mover Tool** icon on the tool palette. Not only does the icon highlight, but an additional sixth menu selection, **Mass Mover,** appears at the right end of the menu. If you click on a measure in

the score, an additional seventh menu choice, **Mass Edit,** will appear at
the right of the menu.

The Drill Icon

When you see the icon Ⓓ , the following information will present a drill that will
clarify one of Finale's commands. Simply follow the numbered steps to complete
each drill.

The Measure Tool

The **Measure Tool** 🗏 is selected by clicking its icon in the Main Tool
Palette. It adds new blank measures at the end of the score, inserting or
deleting measures for all of the staves at the same time. The measure tool
also creates and modifies measure numbers.

1-A Using the Measure Tool

1. Click the Measure Tool 🗏.
2. Select the Measure command in the main Finale menu, and Add from
   the pull down options.
3. A dialog box will appear which asks, "How many measures?" (see Figure
   1-9 [A]). In this dialog box you specify how many measures are to be
   added to the end of your score. Type 11 (do not spell out the word
   eleven, but use the number keys).

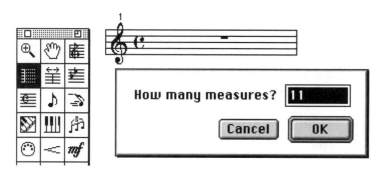

Figure 1-9(A)

4. Click OK or press the Return key. Now you have added additional measures to all your staves in the score or multiple staves created with the Document Setup Wizard.

Remember, when the program is launched, Finale defaults to an untitled window containing one or more measures and one staff, or multiple staves created with the Document Setup Wizard.

There is another special mouse click available with this tool. Option-click the Measure Tool icon/right mouse click to bring up the Add Measure dialog box. In addition, double clicking the measure tool icon add one additional measure.

5. Let's add notation to these new measures. Select the **Simple Note Entry Tool** ♪ . A new palette will appear called, appropriately enough, the **Simple Entry Palette**. After selecting the appropriate note duration, you simply point and click to place notes in your score (see Figure 1-9 [B]).

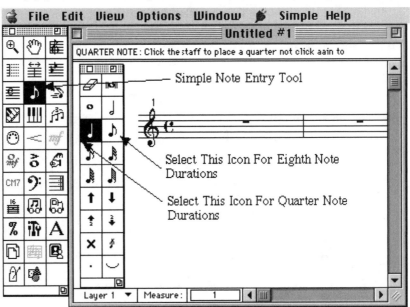

Figure 1-9(B)

The pointer will turn into a crosshair to help you accurately place your notes. When you run out of room, use the horizontal scroll bar to access hidden measures. If you make a mistake, select the **Eraser Tool** and click above the note in the staff to remove it.

5. Add the notes in Figure 1-9 (C) to your score.

Figure 1-9(C)

Always start your score data input in Scroll View, as the computer can redraw the screen more quickly with this view. The slower Page View is best used later, when you are ready to format your score for print output.

Viewing the Score

Finale offers you the choice of two screen views of your music score: **Scroll View**, where the music is presented as an uninterrupted horizontal band, and **Page View**, where you see the music laid out in sheet music form, one page at a time. Finale's tools work equally well in both views.

* Choose Page View from the View menu, or use ⌘-**tilde(~)**/Ctrl+E. Finale reformats the screen to show you the music layout in page format.

Page View

Figure 1-10 shows the elements for navigation in the Page View window. Use ⌘-**tilde(~)**/Ctrl+E to change from Page View to Scroll View without utilizing the mouse. When you use this combination, you will be able to **toggle** between Page View and Scroll View easily.

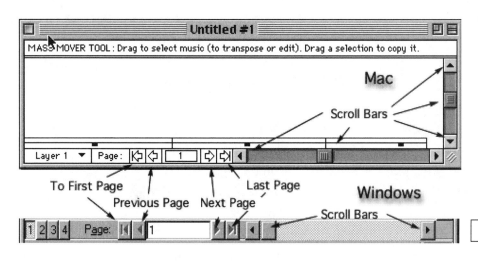

Figure 1-10

Scroll View

The Scroll View score display has been called Igor's View, as a tribute to Igor Stravinsky, who worked at his piano on large scrolls of score paper as he composed. Figure 1-11 contains the necessary information for navigation when in Scroll View.

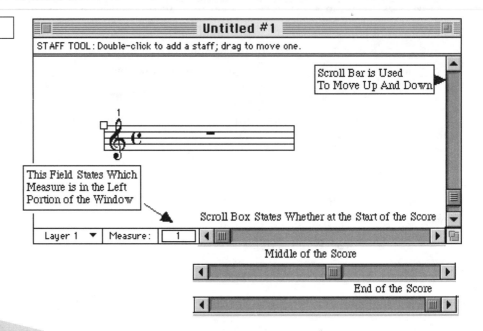

Figure 1-11

If you are working with an extremely large score, you may want to reduce your window size (only showing the staff you are working on) to speed up Finale's operation.

Note that the box in the horizontal scroll bar represents your position in the score. By clicking in this box and dragging it to the left or right, the measure counter will update the measure number when you release the button. Slide the box all the way to the left, and the counter will say 1. Therefore, when you release the mouse button, you will be back at the beginning of the score. You can also click with the mouse on the left or right arrow to advance one measure in the direction clicked. Keep in mind that the window can be resized to show variable amounts of your score, so you can reduce the window to focus on one musical staff at a time.

In Scroll View, imagine that your music is on a long scroll without any separate pages, so the above technique is extremely helpful to go to a specific point in the score. This view is most important for note, articulation, and other detailed entry tasks. Keep in mind that it is very easy to move from one view to the other with Finale.

Redrawing the Screen

Redraw Screen is a special function in the View menu. As Finale is a graphics-intensive program that places great demands on your computer's processor, the performance speed would be greatly reduced if every operation required a screen redraw. With the Redraw Screen command, you can tell Finale to redraw the screen only when you need to fill in a missing portion of the screen, update notational input, or remove a deleted articulation, slur, etc. from the screen (see Figures 1-12 and 1-13).

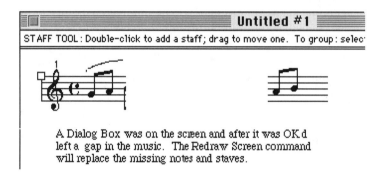

A Dialog Box was on the screen and after it was OK'd left a gap in the music. The Redraw Screen command will replace the missing notes and staves.

Figure 1-12

Figure 1-13

After using the Redraw screen command.

The **Redraw Screen** command can be selected from the View menu, or you can use the ⌘-**D**/Ctrl+D keys on the alphanumeric keyboard.

Try the Redraw Screen command before troubleshooting. It is a very good starting point if you are experiencing any type of difficulty or confusion when inputting or editing musical data with Finale.

Home Position/End Position

Home Position is a simple command that allows you to return to the Home Position, the first measure of the score.

The Home Position command can be selected from the View menu, or by using the ⌘-**H**/Home keys on the alphanumeric keyboard.

The End Position allows you to advance to the final measure of the score Shift-⌘-**H**/End key.

In addition, extended alpha numeric keyboards have individual home and end keys.

Scaling the View

The amount of music viewable on the computer display is dependent on the size of your monitor; therefore, unless your computer has a large screen, you are constrained to its limitations. Finale offers many options to manipulate the view size of a score, such as selecting the **Zoom Tool** 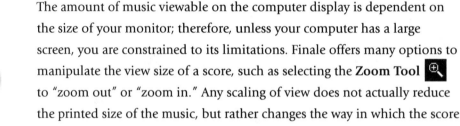 to "zoom out" or "zoom in." Any scaling of view does not actually reduce the printed size of the music, but rather changes the way in which the score is displayed.

1-B Using the Scale View To Command

1. Drag the mouse down the View menu to the **Scale View To** command. Do not release the mouse button yet!

2. Position the cursor on "Scale View To." A submenu will pop out to the right (see Figure 1-14 [A]).

3. Slide the cursor onto the submenu until "75%" is highlighted. Release the mouse button. The window's music is reduced to 75% of its original size so that you can see more of the music.

4. Use the same procedure to select other Scale View percentages from the View menu.

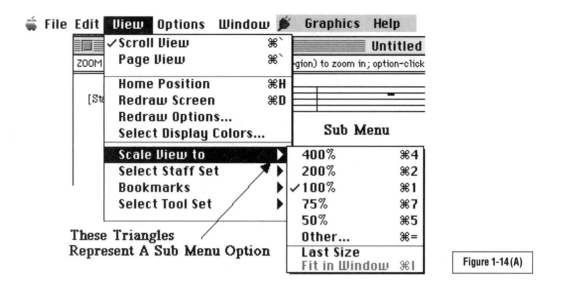

These Triangles
Represent A Sub Menu Option

Figure 1-14 (A)

View Techniques

Reducing the view (less than 100%) can create an overview of your work, allowing access to a greater amount of music for editing.

Enlarging the view (greater than 100%) increases the size of the music score, allowing precision placement of notes, articulations, etc.

Viewing at 100% allows a WYSIWYG (what you see is what you get) view of your score that is the same size as printing output.

When you use the Command/Ctrl key with certain number keys, as shown in Figure 1-14 (B), you can change the scale of your view, eliminating the use of the mouse.

⌘-2/Ctrl +2 = 200%   ⌘-5/Ctrl +5 = 50%

⌘-1/Ctrl +1 = 100%   ⌘-0/Ctrl +0 = ⟵

⌘-7/Ctrl +7 = 75%   (zero)   User Specified
                                      View Percentage

Figure 1-14 (B)

- Try each of the above Scale View power key shortcuts.

Viewing Multiple Windows

Finale lets you open two or more windows displaying the same document. In the other windows, you can vary the view from the first by zooming in, zooming out, switching to either Page View or Scroll View, and so on. Keep in mind that new windows are *not* different copies of your music, but independent views of the same piece. Therefore, changes made in one window will be updated in the document and any other open window.

- From the Window menu, choose **New Window**.

A new window will appear containing the opened Finale document. Each additional window will be sequentially numbered and can be selected from the bottom of the Window menu (see Figure 1-14 [C]), or clicked on the screen to become active.

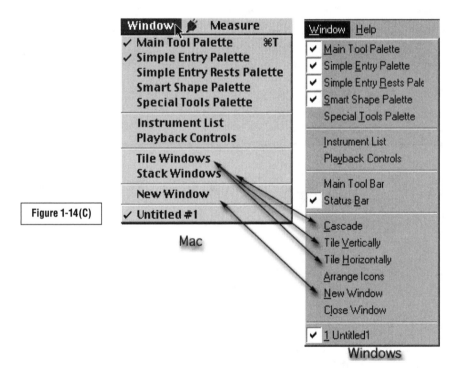

Figure 1-14(C)

- In the active window choose the Scale View To submenu of the View menu, and choose 200%. Now you have two windows—one at double size, and the other window at a reduced view.

Suppose you decide that the active window contains the view you really want to work on, and you would like it to fill your screen—but you still want access to the other window. Enter the stacking window option.

Stacking Windows

You are not limited to two windows. It is possible to have as many windows open as desired. In fact, they do not have to be a window of the same document—you can open multiple documents, too, each in its own window and with its own independent magnification, RAM permitting.

• Choose **Stack Windows/Cascade** from the Window menu.

Finale arranges the windows so that the active window fills the screen, but you can still see the background window(s) around the edges. A click on any of these edges will bring that window to the front. The active window will always be topmost when windows are stacked (see Figure 1-15).

Figure 1-15

• From the Scale View To submenu of the View menu, choose 100%. The score returns to its normal size.

The ability to access the contents of two or more windows at once often makes for efficient music input.

Tiling Windows

Finale offers an alternative way to view multiple windows called **tiling**. With tiled windows, all open windows are placed *contiguously* on the screen. That is, each window falls underneath the first one, each resized to equally fit within the screen (see Figure 1-16). If you use the Close box to eliminate one or several windows, use the Zoom box on the remaining window(s) to expand it to full screen size.

• Make sure that you have three windows open by using the New Window command from the Window menu.

- From the Window menu choose **Tile Windows/Tile Horizontally** or **Tile Vertically.**

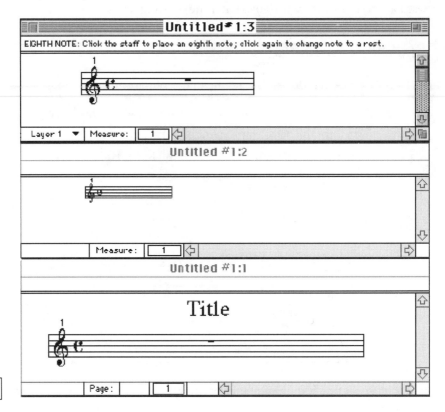

Figure 1-16

By observing the thin horizontal lines in the **title bar** of a window, you can always see which window is active.

Closing All Windows

If you hold down the Option key and select the Close box in any Finale window, all open windows will immediately close. This action is not available in Windows.

You now know how to either stack or tile windows when needed.

Saving Your Work

When you open a document, the computer transfers its information from the hard disk drive or floppy disk into its RAM memory. As you work with a score, all changes exist only in this temporary memory area. If someone trips on the computer's power cord, or the computer should go into a system hang, all of your work will be lost. You will be left only with what was originally saved before your current input. Therefore:

It is important to save your work at regular intervals.

Save every 15 minutes or so. This way, if you encounter problems, you will only lose 15 minutes of working time, as opposed to your entire Finale session.

Remember, there are two types of computer users: those who lose data and those who will lose data!

Saving to Disk

- Choose **Save** from the File menu (or press ⌘-**S**)/Ctrl+S. The dialog box in Figure 1-17 will appear.

You can now save your new score or updated changes on floppy disk or the computer's hard disk. For now, be sure the **radio button** ◉ Standard Finale File in the Type dialog box area is selected, or the file type flyout in Windows. Figure 1-17(B).

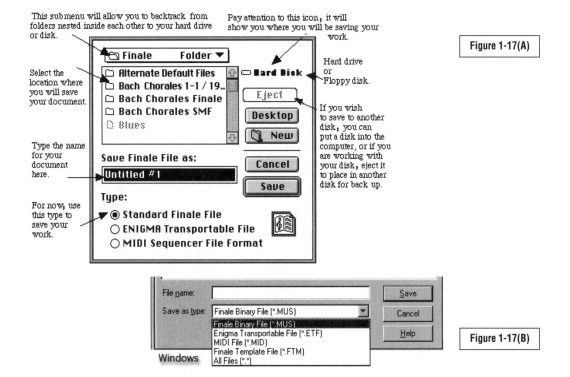

Figure 1-17(A)

Figure 1-17(B)

Saving to Your Disk and to Other Locations

Back up your work by using the **Save As** command in the File menu. Save As will allow you to create a new document of your existing work without affecting the document you have opened (see Figure 1-17).

You can save different versions of your score or back up the same document to another disk. If you are afraid you might forget to save your work, running the risk of losing your changes in the event of a power or computer system failure, consider using Finale's automatic backup feature, Auto Save.

Auto Save

Finale has a very convenient feature called **Auto Save**. When you activate this option, Finale will automatically save your document at a user defined interval in a folder that you predetermine.

To activate this feature, simply pull down the **Options** menu and select **Program Options** as pictured in Figure 1-18.

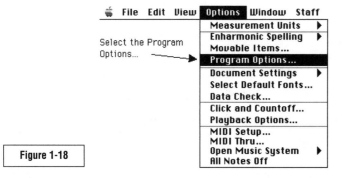

Figure 1-18

You will be presented with a dialog box, illustrated in Figure 1-19. Turn Auto Save on by selecting this option, then type in the time lapse between saves (I recommend 15 minutes).

Use the Select Folder button to specify to which folder Finale will Auto Save your work.

Closing, Opening, and Quitting

Check The Auto Save Option

Select A Folder In Which Your Work Will Be Saved

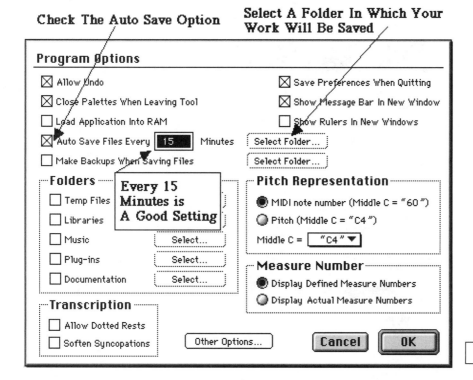

Program Options

☒ Allow Undo

☒ Close Palettes When Leaving Tool

☐ Load Application Into RAM

☒ Auto Save Files Every [15] Minutes

☐ Make Backups When Saving Files

☒ Save Preferences When Quitting

☒ Show Message Bar In New Window

☐ Show Rulers In New Windows

Select Folder...

Select Folder...

Every 15 Minutes is A Good Setting

Folders

☐ Temp Files

☐ Libraries

☐ Music   Select...

☐ Plug-ins   Select...

☐ Documentation   Select...

Transcription

☐ Allow Dotted Rests

☐ Soften Syncopations

Other Options...

Pitch Representation

⦿ MIDI note number (Middle C = "60")

◯ Pitch (Middle C = "C4")

Middle C = ["C4" ▼]

Measure Number

⦿ Display Defined Measure Numbers

◯ Display Actual Measure Numbers

Cancel   OK

Figure 1-19

Use the **Close** command, ⌘-**W**/Ctrl+W from the File menu when you wish to exit a Finale document but still have the application remain open (see Figure 1-20).

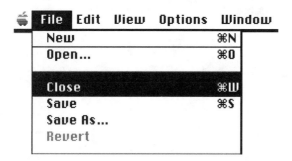

| File | Edit | View | Options | Window |

New   ⌘N

Open...   ⌘O

Close   ⌘W

Save   ⌘S

Save As...

Revert

Figure 1-20

Select the New command, Command-N ⌘-**N**/Ctrl+N if you wish to create a new Finale document (see Figure 1-21). An Untitled window will appear on your screen.

Figure 1-21

 Select the Open command, ⌘-**O**/Ctrl+O to open an existing Finale document (see Figure 1-22).

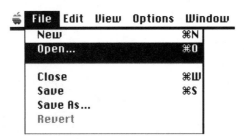

Figure 1-22

The following dialog box will appear for selecting a document to open (Figure 1-23).

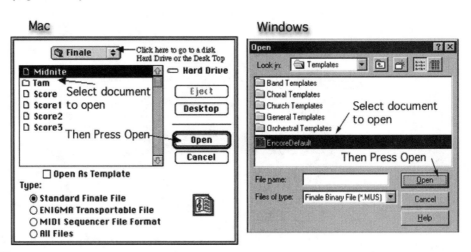

Figure 1-23

Open As Template

Templates in Finale are time-saving files that have been previously formatted and saved without musical data. Templates will only contain page layout information such as proper number of staves, staff names and groupings, etc. The user will then input the musical data and save as another document. Examples of templates are: two staves for piano music, a guitar staff with tablature, big band score, or string quartet score. Each one of these can be opened at the beginning of a notation project to eliminate the time required to lay out your score.

Finale comes with a wide array of templates that are loaded into your computer. Find the Templates folder in your Finale folder and open it. Figure 1-24(B) shows you some of the template files available.

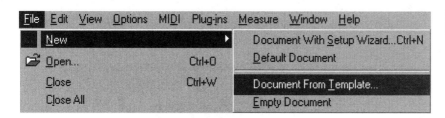

Figure 1-24(A)

Figure 1-24(B)

Whenever you are working with templates in Finale, always make sure that the Document from Template Command is used. See figure 1-25. This will maintain the template you are opening as a template, which means that you will not replace the blank template with notation input when saved.

Figure 1-25

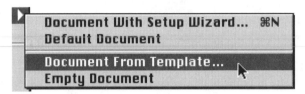

1-C Using Open As Template

1. Select New from File main menu

2. From the flyout triangle select Document Fom Template.

3. Find and open the Finale folder.

4. Find and open the folder named Templates.

5. Open the various templates that are available. Study several of the existing templates for future use when starting a Finale document.

If you have opened a template without selecting the Document From Template command, make sure you use the Save As command so that you do not save inputted notes in a template. If you wish to create and save a unique template, design and save it in the Templates folder.

If you have not saved your work, closing a single existing window of your score will signal Finale to quit. This gives you the option of saving the changes, discarding them, or leaving the document as it was when it was last saved.

To quit the program, select the command Quit, ⌘-**Q**/Alt+F4 (see Figure 1-26).

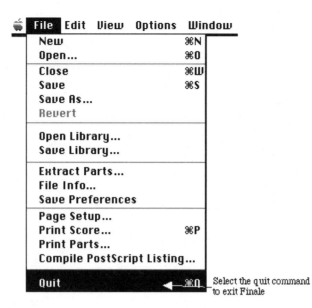

Figure 1-26

Select the quit command
to exit Finale

Some computer monitors will not display all the commands from the
File menu. If this is your situation, a small arrow will be at the bottom of
the Command list. By dragging the pointer to and below this arrow, you
can select commands that are hidden (see Figure 1-27).

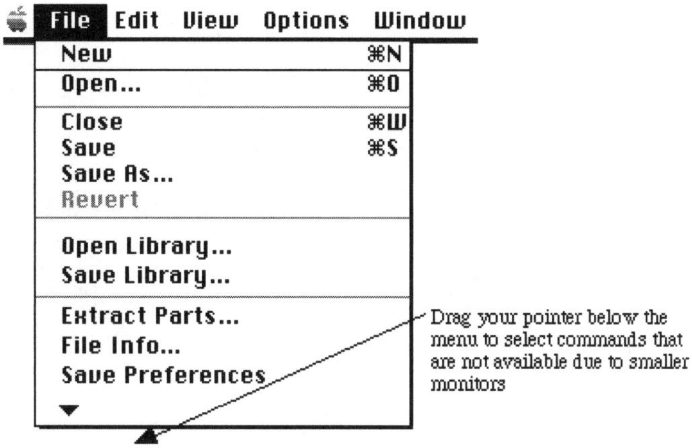

Drag your pointer below the
menu to select commands that
are not available due to smaller
monitors

Figure 1-27

Chapter One Review

Using the commands covered so far, you now know how to manipulate and control the view of your work in the following ways:

Use the View menu to select Page View or Scroll View

Use the Scale To Percentage to zoom in or zoom out

Use the Window menu to add additional windows

Use the Window menu's Tile and Stack Windows commands

Save your work

Use Auto Save

Open existing documents

Open a document from template

Close and quit Finale

Review the material if you cannot do any of the above options, and be sure to learn all the presented power keystrokes.

Notes:

The Finale Toolbox

Finale uses an approach frequently encountered in computer graphics programs, which is a combination of a tool palette and menu interfaces to access all of the commands for creating a document. The tool palette remains on the desktop within easy reach of the user for selecting a tool. Finale's tools allow for creating and editing all aspects of notation such as key signatures, time signatures, notes and rests, etc. Let's explore the basic Finale tools, and their use in creating a score.

When you click on a tool, two things occur:

Instructions regarding the use of the tool appear at the top of the page when the message bar is active or at the bottom of the screen when the status bar is active.

A new menu option(s) appears in the menu bar, which is designed for use with that tool.

The Staff

The staff is the most basic of all the music symbols, for it serves as the locale for almost all the other signs in music notation. Note elements (note-heads, stems, flags, and beams) must be positioned on a staff; accidentals, rests, bar-lines, and time signatures must also be accommodated by its lines and spaces. Even accents, dynamics, and phrase marks are placed in relation to the notes they affect, and so are dependent on the staff for proper notation.

—From the book *Music Notation* by Gardner Read, pp. 27-28

Finale will default to one staff and one measure when launched, but over 400 staves are possible in a score. Multiple or single staves can be repositioned simply by Shift-clicking and dragging. Total control of all staff characteristics such as spacing and multiple bracket selections allow you to create custom scores and staves, including a single line staff for rhythm, or tablature for guitar notation. Multi-voices of rhythmically independent musical lines can reside on one staff. It is also possible to place staves on different MIDI channels to create a performance where each staff plays back a different timbre, enabling a virtual performance of your composition or arrangement.

The Staff Tool

In Finale 2000 and above, when you select the **Staff Tool** from the Main Tool Palette, you will be able to control the number and placement of staves within your score. The usual shape of the pointer will change into a crosshair + for Mac / + for Windows once the Staff Tool is selected to allow greater accuracy when adding or repositioning staves in your document.

The Staff Tool has two levels of utilization, rudimentary (mouse-activated commands) and more complex (menu-activated commands). The following are important rudimentary functions where only the mouse is necessary:

Add a new staff by double-clicking in the document window where you want a new staff to appear, either above or below the existing staff(s).

Reposition a staff by clicking in its handle (see Figure 2-1) and dragging. Be aware that it is possible to place one staff on top of another in very special cases.

An important term to understand when working with Finale is **Systems**. A system is a collection of two or more staves.

Adding Staves

- Open a new Finale document and select the Staff Tool from the Main Tool Palette.

- Move the cursor an inch or two below the existing staff and double-click on the mouse; a second staff will appear.

- Add four staves to your document.

It is simple to add staves in Finale: click the Staff Tool and double-click anywhere on the screen.

Editing Staves

When the Staff Tool is selected, all staves in the score have a **handle** (a small box in the upper left-hand staff line). It is not a very large target, but with practice you will be able to select a staff with ease. You can always tell when a staff is selected, because its handle will be highlighted in black.

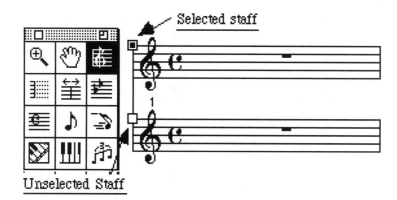

Figure 2-1

To *remove a staff*, simply select its handle by clicking on it, and press the Delete key / Delete key.

Select the three staves using the Shift-click technique and press the Delete key. This will remove all the staves.

- Now practice *repositioning the staves* in your score.

Selecting Multiple Staves

An easy way to select multiple staves is by using the *marquee technique*. Position the crosshair pointer to the left of the handle of the uppermost stave you wish to select as a group. Drag the mouse diagonally to the right to create a **marquee,** a dotted rectangular box. When you have enclosed all the handles for the staves you wish to group, simply release the mouse to select them (see Figure 2-2). Multiple staves can also be selected by holding the Shift key and clicking in the staff select handles.

When a staff or staves are selected, you can move them horizontally or vertically by clicking in the selected handle and dragging.

To select *noncontiguous* staves (ones that are not next to each other) you must use the Shift-click approach. If you select multiple staves with the marquee method, use the Shift-click method to de-select unwanted staves that were included in the marquee (see Figure 2-3).

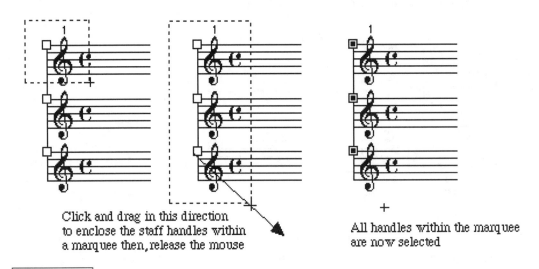

Click and drag in this direction to enclose the staff handles within a marquee then, release the mouse

All handles within the marquee are now selected

Figure 2-2

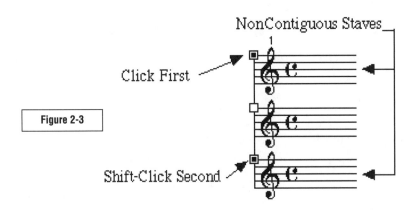

NonContiguous Staves

Click First

Shift-Click Second

Figure 2-3

- Use a marquee to drag-enclose the handles of multiple staves you wish to select.

- Experiment with either repositioning or deleting them.

- To de-select any staff handle, simply click on a spot in the window that is not a staff handle.

Shift-clicking will toggle between selecting a staff and de-selecting a staff when the marquee technique is used.

If you find you have moved a staff rather than selected it, you can go to the Edit menu in the main Finale menu and select **Undo,** or use the keyboard shortcut ⌘-**Z** / Ctrl + **Z**. *This will undo every action you have taken since opening a Finale document.* ⌘-**Y** / Ctrl + **Y** will redo every action you have taken since opening a Finale document.

Menu-Activated Staff Commands

When you select some of the tools in the Main Tool Palette, an additional pull-down menu item(s) will appear in the main menu bar (see Figure 2-4 [A]). There is a redundancy of commands between the menu commands using the mouse and power keys, but there are also additional powerful editing and score layout commands in the main menu not available with power keys.

Figure 2-4 (A)

Study Figure 2-4 (B), which illustrates all the additional intricate editing possibilities available with the Staff Tool.

New Staves -- adds one or multiple staves beneath the existing staff or staves.

New Staves (with Setup Wizard) -- brings up the Setup Wizard sequence for adding staves.

Delete Staves -- available when more than one staff is in the score. Select the staff or staves for deletion, and the remaining staves will retain the same place in the score, creating a gap in the score.

Delete Staves and Reposition -- available when more than one staff is in the score. Select the staff or staves for deletion, and the remaining staves will repositon to the staff directly above the deleted ones.

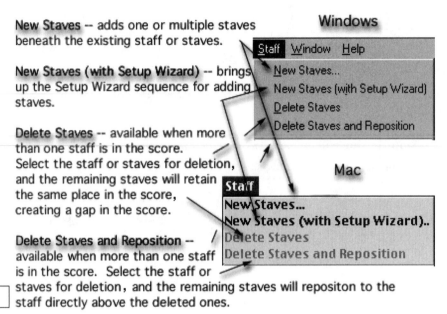

Figure 2-4(B)

When you select the **Add Staves** or **Insert Staves** commands, a dialog box will appear to select the number of staves added (1 to 400+) (see figure 2-4[C]).

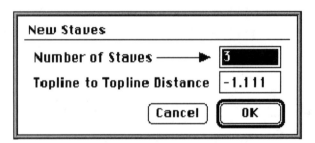

Figure 2-4(C)

The **Delete Staves** and **Delete Staves and Reposition** commands do not have dialog boxes but are executed immediately upon selection.

In Finale, positive numbers measure upward; negative numbers measure downward.

- Practice adding, inserting, deleting, and deleting and repositioning staves from the Staff Tool menu. Use both the Shift key and marquee technique to select multiple staves.

- Use the View Menu and select show rulers to make the task of adjusting staves easier. ⌘-R / not available in Windows. This will show rulers around the window. Use the hide ruler command to get rid of rulers. Windows users can go to the View menu and select theShow Rulers command.

Edit Staff Attributes

When you double-click anywhere on a staff (to the right of the time signature), or select the **Edit Staff Attributes** command (from the Staff menu) you will be able to edit and specify staff attributes for every individual staff via the Staff Attributes dialog box. These attributes include:

The name of the instrument

Automatic transposition (if it's a trumpet or clarinet staff, for example)

Alternate notation

Rest and barline display

The specific number of lines in a staff, from 0 to 100

The ability to display or hide specific musical elements in a staff (measure numbers, expression markings, time signatures, etc.)

Study the Staff Attributes dialog box in Figures 2-5 through 2-7, and you can see the logic of how it determines the attributes for a staff.

Remember, if the score does not look exactly the way you want it, you can use the Command-Z power key routine to execute the Undo function.

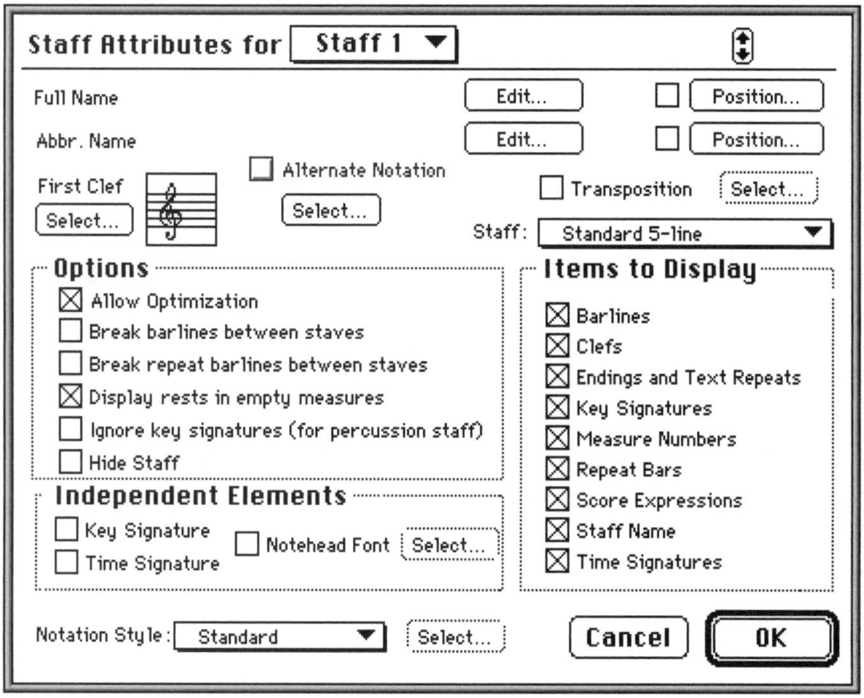

Figure 2-5

A pull-down menu where you specify which staff of a system the
Staff Attributes dialog box will control

Figure 2-6

When multiple staves are present in a score these arrows can move you to the next staff above or below to set the staff attributes.

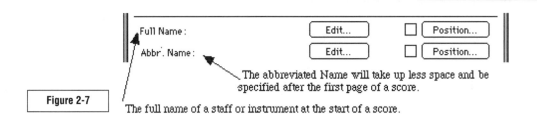

The abbreviated Name will take up less space and be specified after the first page of a score.

Figure 2-7

The full name of a staff or instrument at the start of a score.

Staff names are created when you click the button and type the name in the Edit Text dialog box that will appear as illustrated in Figure 2-8.

Figure 2-8

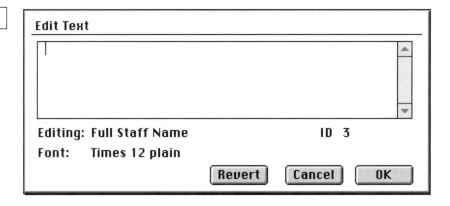

When you are typing in a name in the Edit Text dialog box, do not use the Return key to OK your finished name, as this is interpreted as a new paragraph return only.

Once Full Staff Names or Abbreviated Names are entered, they will always appear in the Staff Attributes dialog box.

Entering a Staff Name

- Select the Staff Tool and double-click anywhere after the time signature in one of the staves. The Staff Attributes dialog box will appear. Make sure that the pop-up menu at the top of the dialog box says Staff 1 (see Figure 2-9 [A]).

Figure 2-9(A)

- Select the **Edit...** button for Full Staff Name and type Soprano in the Edit Text dialog box.

- Use the same procedure to enter Sop. as its Abbr. (Abbreviated) Name. Click the Position Button and then adjust the positioning of the Full Staff Name in the dialog box that appears (see Figure 2-9 [B]).

- Click OK. The new positioning of the Staff Name will be reflected in your score.

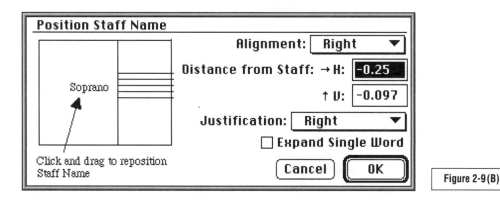

Figure 2-9(B)

Notice that the box before Position now contains an X, ☒ **Position...** , informing you that you have moved the position of the name from its default.

If you are sharing a staff name between two staves, you will have to push the name out of the window view either above or below the selected staff to achieve the desired result. Then go back to your score to check positioning results.

If you click on a staff name's handle, you can reposition the name by simply dragging it to a new position in the score (see Figure 2-10).

Figure 2-10

Setting the Name Font

When you click the [Edit...] button and the Edit Text dialog box appears, notice that the word Text is now in the main menu bar. To edit a staff name or abbreviation, simply highlight your staff name and use the pull-down menu for standard text editing such as font, size, style, etc. The abbreviated name adjusts in the same manner (see Figure 2-11 [A]).

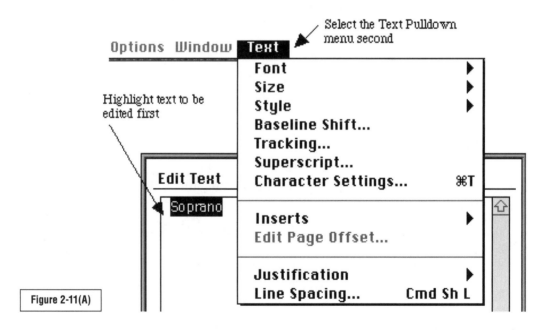

Figure 2-11(A)

- From the pop-up menu at the top of the dialog box, choose Staff 2 (see Figure 2-11 [B]). The contents of the dialog box change to reflect the staff attributes of the second staff in the score.

- Name this Alto and enter Alt. as its abbreviated name.

Figure 2-11(B)

- If there were more than two staves, you would continue to access their attributes boxes by selecting their name in the pop-up menu, without having to return to the score.

Choosing the Clef Sign

Most instruments are notated in one clef only, regardless of the amount of ledger lines required for high or low pitches. A few instruments, such as horn, piano, or cello, permit the use of more than one clef to make such extreme pitches easy to read.

The **Clef Tool** 𝄢 allows you to change the clef *after the first clef in a score;* the Staff Attributes dialog box always establishes the first clef for each staff (see Figure 2-12 [A]).

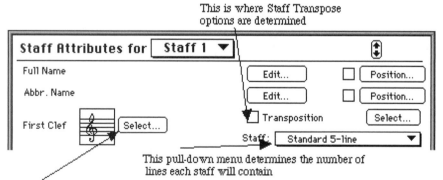

Figure 2-12(A)

Transposing Instruments and Finale

If you are working with a full score containing transposing instruments, it is very important that you let Finale know about their presence. Finale has a great feature that allows you to select the way you want to display transposing instrument parts either at concert pitch or their transposition.

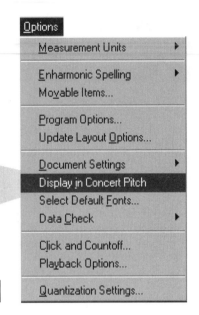

Select Options in the main menu and select Display in Concert Pitch. This option helps you work with a score the way that is easiest for you. When you enter notes for a transposed instrument at the concert pitch it will automatically transpose when you select display in Concert Pitch again.

When you start a new document the simplest way to establish transposing instruments is to use the Setup Wizard. When you pick a transposing instrument the Setup Wizard automatically sets the appropriate transposition. Transposing after a staff is entered is possible but not as efficient.

When this command has a check beside it, you are viewing the score in concert pitch.

Figure 2-12(B)

Transposing Instruments

If you have a transposing instrument in your score, such as the ones in Project 5 at the end of this chapter, you will need to check the Transposition Box in the Staff Attributes dialog box (see Figure 2-12 [C]).

Figure 2-12(C)

Once you have selected the transpose option for this staff, click on the Select button next to it to bring up the Staff Transpositions dialog box in

Figure 2-12 (D). When you choose the proper transposition for this instrument, it will affect only that staff and not all instruments in the score.

See Appendix 9 and 10 for a Conventional Instrument Transposition Chart and Score Order Chart on pp. 245-248.

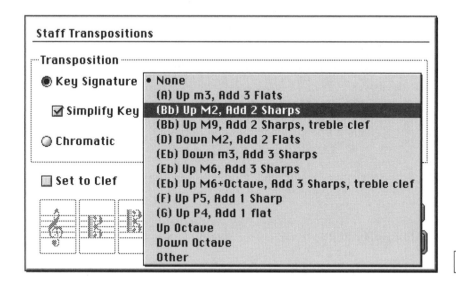

Figure 2-12(D)

Display Options

If there is an X in any of the boxes for Options or Items to Display, then those options or items will take effect or be displayed for that staff respectively (see Figure 2-13).

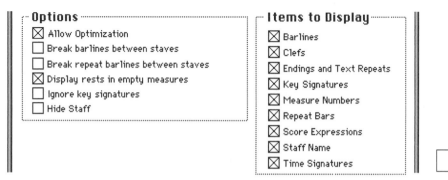

Figure 2-13

Independent Elements

When Independent Elements boxes contain an X, these elements are allowed to vary from staff to staff. Therefore, if Time Signature was selected, a different meter is possible from staff to staff in the score. This is also true for other independent elements (see Figure 2-14).

Simply press the Return key, Enter key or click on the OK button in the dialog box when you have established all the independent elements for your score's staves.

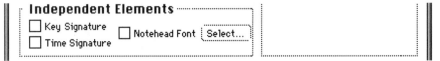

Figure 2-14

2-A Staff Attributes Drill

1. Open a new document and place two staves on the page using the Staff Tool.

2. Double-click anywhere on the second staff.

3. Next to the word First Clef, click Select. Finale will display a graphic palette containing a selection of clefs (see Figure 2-15).

4. Double-click the bass clef (upper right).

5. You will return to the Staff Attributes box, and Finale now displays a bass clef (Figure 2-16).

6. Just click OK, press the Return key or press Enter, and you have just created the beginning of a piano (grand) staff.

Within the Staff Attributes dialog box, the Staff field will specify the number of lines that will be present for each staff within a system (0-100).

To change a staff's number of lines, simply select one of the pull-down menu items in Figure 2-17.

The five-line staff was first used in the early thirteenth century for vocal polyphonic music. The five-line staff did not become standard for all music

Be careful that you do not select the wrong clef for a staff, such as the Tenor-voice clef or Double-bass clef for the G-clef or Bass clef. Carefully study the clef names illustrated in Figure 2-15.

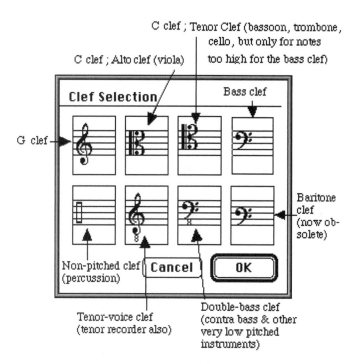

C clef ; Tenor Clef (bassoon, trombone, cello, but only for notes too high for the bass clef)

C clef ; Alto clef (viola)

Bass clef

G clef —

Baritone clef (now obsolete)

Non-pitched clef (percussion)

Tenor-voice clef (tenor recorder also)

Double-bass clef (contra bass & other very low pitched instruments)

Figure 2-15

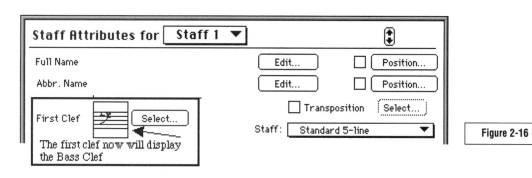

Staff Attributes for Staff 1 ▼

Full Name   Edit...   ☐ Position...
Abbr. Name   Edit...   ☐ Position...
             ☐ Transposition Select...
First Clef   Select...
             Staff: Standard 5-line ▼

The first clef now will display the Bass Clef

Figure 2-16

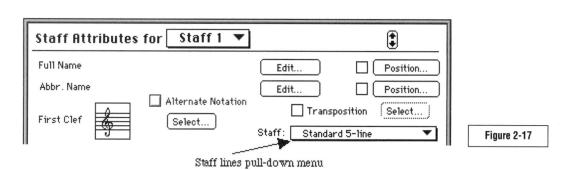

Staff Attributes for Staff 1 ▼

Full Name   Edit...   ☐ Position...
Abbr. Name   Edit...   ☐ Position...
             ☐ Alternate Notation
First Clef   Select... ☐ Transposition Select...
             Staff: Standard 5-line ▼

Staff lines pull-down menu

Figure 2-17

The Finale Toolbox   49

until the mid-seventeenth century. A staff consisting of four lines was widely used from the eleventh to thirteenth centuries. Some keyboard music of the sixteenth and seventeenth centuries employed as many as fifteen lines. But such large staves were unwieldy, and were gradually replaced by the present five-line staff.

—From *Music Notation* by Gardner Read, pp. 27-28

Figure 2-18 shows Finale's staff setup options.

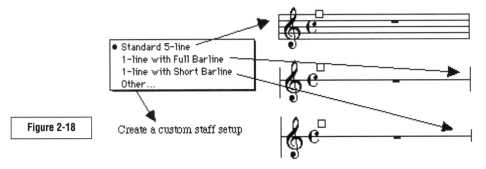

Figure 2-18

2-B Creating a Single-Line Staff and Percussion Clef

1. Create the following single-line staff and percussion clef for the second staff in your score (Figure 2-19).

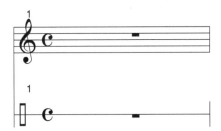

Figure 2-19

2. Now revert back to the five-line staff and bass clef (Figure 2-20).

Figure 2-20

The Add Group and Bracket Command and the Staff Tool

The **Add Group and Bracket** command is the first step for placing braces and brackets into your score. The *brace* and *bracket* give scores an organized visual pattern for reading music. When two or more staves are present in a score, it is called a system—a group of staves, each with individual clef-signs, designed to be read simultaneously rather than one by one.

The brace is used to connect such elements as the two or more staves of a keyboard (synthesizer, organ, celesta, and harpsichord) or harp. The staves are further joined by a single vertical line following the brace sign (see Figure 2-21).

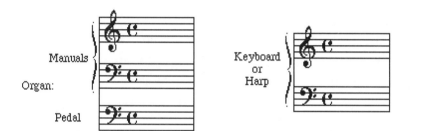

Figure 2-21

The bracket *most commonly functions to connect such basically individual lines as the four staves of a string quartet score or the several staves of a choral work. Again a single vertical line joins all the staves; somewhat thicker than the brace, with thin curved ends extending above and below the outer staves. It is customary to use the bracket rather than the bow-shaped brace to group two or more staves bearing quite separate or individual parts, whether vocal or instrumental.*

—From *Music Notation* by Gardner Read, pp. 35-37

Figure 2-22 illustrates two bracket options available with Finale 2000 (see next page).

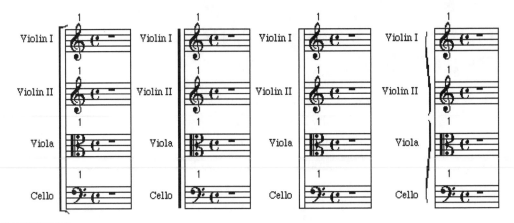

Figure 2-22

Group and Staff Names

Staff and group names are completely user-defined and editable. Look at
Figure 2-23 (A) to see the default names that a new Finale document
provides. If you do not wish to have the default group or staff names
present, first select either the **Show Default Staff** or **Group** names in the
Staff menu commands. The commands will then be able to toggle to
display the names or not. A check to the right means that either the staff or

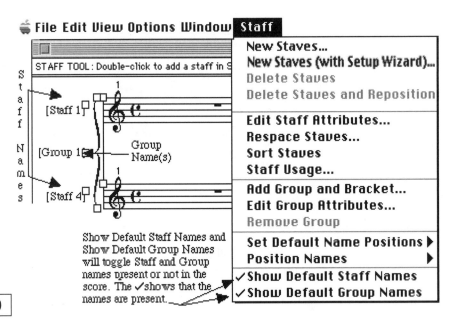

Figure 2-23(A)

the group name is present, and nondisplay of a check means that the name will not be present.

Grouping Staves with the Staff Tool

The Staff Tool is used to group staves so that the barlines will continue through from one staff to another (see Figure 2-23 [B]).

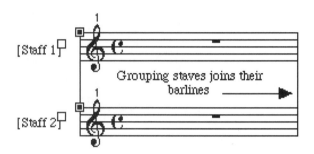

Figure 2-23(B)

When you select the Add Group and Bracket command from the Staff menu as in Figure 2-23 (C), a Group Attributes dialog box will appear. This dialog box is very similar to the Staff Attributes dialog box; editing features such as Full Group Name and Abbr. Group Name function exactly the same.

The Group Attributes dialog box allows staves to be grouped and bracketed according to a score's demands. Use of a Group Attributes dialog box for grouping and bracketing makes creating complex orchestral scores fairly simple with easy click-and-drag graphic style selection and placement. Study Figure 2-24 (A) to become familiar with the options available in this dialog box.

Figure 2-23(C)

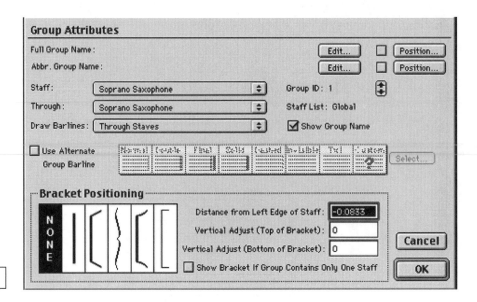

Figure 2-24(A)

You can change the Group Name or Abbr. Name by simply clicking the
[Edit...] button and addressing the same edit sequence in the Edit Text
dialog box as with Staff Names (see Figure 2-24 [B]).

Figure 2-24(B)

Group Attributes

Full Group Name :   [Edit...] ☐ [Position...]
Abbr. Group Name :   [Edit...] ☐ [Position...]

The choices in the Group Attributes dialog box in Figure 2-24 (C) define
the range of staves that the grouping or bracket will address. To define this
range, use the two pop-up menus Staff and Through to pick the staves for
grouping. The Group ID number will increase with each additional
grouping or bracket that you place in the score.

Figure 2-24(C)

Staff :   [Staff 1]   ▼   Group ID: 2   ⬍
Through :   [Staff 2]   ▼   Staff List: Global

In Figure 2-24 (D) you use the Draw Barlines pop-up menu to define the
grouping line that will pass through the staves which you have defined using
Staff and Through. Leave this pop-up menu set to • Through Staves.

An X in this field will permit the appearance of the Group Name:

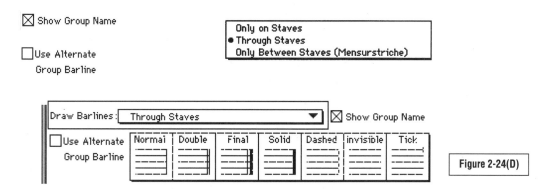

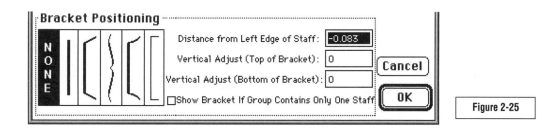

Figure 2-24(D)

If you want to use Alternate Group Barlines, select this option and the style of barline that you desire. Keep in mind that all alternate grouping barlines will apply to every measure in the score.

In Figure 2-25 you can select the required bracket for your score by clicking on one of the bracket options. None is the default setting.

Figure 2-25

You can ungroup staves by selecting the staves that are grouped and selecting the command **Remove Group** from the Staff menu.

2-C Grouping Staves

1. Delete all but two staves by using the Staff Tool.

2. Starting in the blank space above and to the left of the upper staff, drag-enclose both staves' handles and release the mouse button.

3. Go to the Staff menu and select the Add Group and Bracket command.

4. Select OK to group these two staves.

The Finale Toolbox

This can also be done for more than two staves. When staves are grouped they will remain grouped as you add measures.

2-D Building a Grand Staff

1. Delete all but two staves by using the Staff Tool ![staff tool icon].

2. Group the staves together and select their handles.

3. Select the Add Group and Bracket command from the Staff pull-down menu.

4. Click the brace from the Bracket Positioning in the Group Attributes dialog box.

5. When you click OK, a brace will bracket the Grand Staff piano staves.

Editing Brackets

The brace or bracket that you have selected for your score can be moved or resized by dragging the handles (see Figure 2-26).

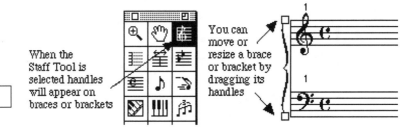

When the Staff Tool is selected handles will appear on braces or brackets

You can move or resize a brace or bracket by dragging its handles

Figure 2-26

You can move a bracket by its handles if the Staff Tool is selected. When you drag the top handle of a bracket horizontally, the entire bracket will move; when you drag either handle vertically it will allow you to make it enclose even nongrouped staves.

The handles will not appear on the screen when another tool is selected.

Nested Brackets

You can create *nested brackets* (additional brackets) after you have grouped staves in the usual way by selecting the stave(s) for nesting and using the Add Group and Bracket command.

When you click the `Group ID: 2` upper arrow to a higher ID number this will permit you to add the desired bracket style for nesting.

If you are using longer brackets for the score and shorter ones for instrument groupings, drag the longer ones to the left with the top bracket handle. These can be dragged to the right once you have completed all smaller nested brackets. Reduce the score view so that you can see a larger portion of the score and work either from the top down or bottom up to expand or reduce the nested brackets (see Figure 2-27).

This is a time-consuming process, so save your work when you finish formatting your score. If you use a complicated score layout, save it often as a template in the template folder.

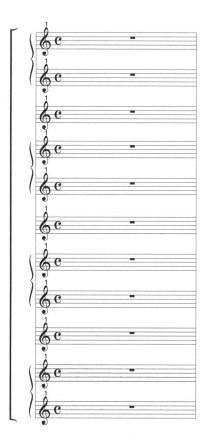

Figure 2-27

Deleting Brackets

If you are having a problem with brackets, select the Staff Tool and the grouped and bracketed staves you wish to delete. Then select Remove Group from the Staff menu. This will clear all selected brackets from your score, and ungroup the selected staves (see Figure 2-28).

To delete a brace or bracket, simply click a handle and press the Delete key.

Staff
Add Staves...
Insert Staves...
Delete Staves
Delete Staves and Reposition
Edit Staff Attributes...
Respace Staves...
Sort Staves
Staff Usage...
Add Group and Bracket...
Edit Group Attributes...
Remove Group

Figure 2-28

2-E Reviewing the Add Group and Bracket Command

1. Create two staves (click the Staff Tool and double-click the screen for each one).

2. Group the staves by selecting both handles and select the Add Group and Bracket command.

3. Add the brace from the Group Attributes dialog box. Click OK.

4. Change the lower staff's clef by double-clicking in the staff to bring up the Staff Attributes dialog box. Click on the Select button in the First Clef field, and click on the desired clef. Then Click OK.

By double-clicking the cursor anywhere on the screen with the Staff Tool, you can add staves one at a time. If you are going to create more complicated scores, you will need to add multiple staves at once with uniform spacing.

Sorting Staves

The **Sort Staves** command will repair any brackets and barlines that have become broken after a score is rearranged (see Figures 2-29 [A] and [B]).

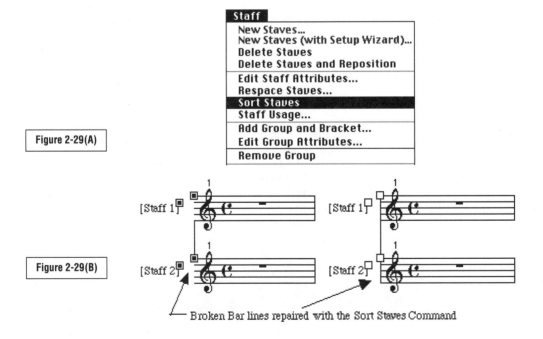

Figure 2-29(A)

Figure 2-29(B)

Broken Bar lines repaired with the Sort Staves Command

Creating and Selecting Staff Sets

When multiple staves are present in a score, screen redraw time can become noticeably slower, especially on an older model computer. You can bypass this dilemma in Scroll View by hiding staves that are not being edited. With Staff Sets, you designate which staves you wish to see without disturbing staff arrangements in the full score. You can have up to eight different Staff Sets in your Finale document in addition to the full score view.

2-F Creating and Naming Staves

1. Create and name six staves as in Figure 2-30.

2. Use the Staff Tool and Edit Staff Attributes commands.

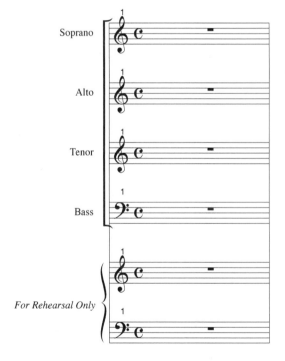

Figure 2-30

Programming Staff Sets

When in Scroll View, you can program Staff Sets, which are views of your score containing only the staves you program from a system. These independent staff sets will allow you to input and edit only on the staves that they contain. Up to eight staff set combinations can be programmed. Follow Drill 2-G to program staff sets.

2-G Programming Staff Sets

1. Select the Staff Tool 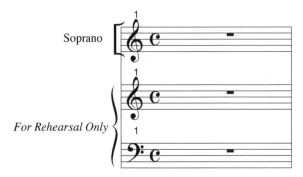.

2. While pressing the Shift key, select the handles of the staves you wish to include in a Staff Set. It does not matter whether or not the staves are adjacent.

3. Choose the Soprano and two For Rehearsal Only staves.

4. Hold down the Option key/right mouse click, and choose **Program Staff Set** from the View menu.

5. Then choose Staff Set 1 from the subset that appears on your screen (see Figure 2-31).

Staff Set 1

Figure 2-31

6. Repeat this process with another combination of staves, and select Staff Set 2—Alto and For Rehearsal Only, Staff Set 3—Tenor and Rehearsal Only, Staff Set 4—Bass and Rehearsal Only, etc. (see Figure 2-32).

Staff Set 4

Figure 2-32

You have now just programmed multiple Staff Sets.

Selecting Staff Sets

You can select Staff Sets in one of two ways. First, simply choose the command **Select Staff Set** from the View menu and pick one of the Staff Set numbers from the submenu (see Figure 2-33).

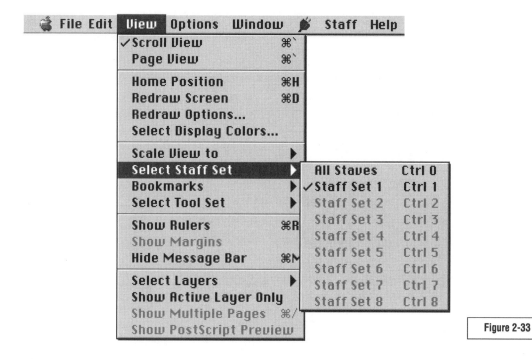

Figure 2-33

The second way of selecting Staff Sets is to press the Control key [ctrl] and a number key 1 through 8 (not available in Windows) to choose the appropriate Staff Set (1 through 8). Control-0 restores the full score view.

The Key Signature Tool

Key signatures are groups of sharps or flats at the start of each staff following the clef sign that affect the pitches they designate in all octaves and all measures (unless there is a change of signatures). Accidentals within a measure are somewhat different in that they affect only the pitches they precede.

Setting the Key Signature

When you click the **Key Signature Tool** ⊞ , a handle appears on every barline of the piece. To change a key signature, click the measure or its handle that you wish to change. The Key Signature dialog box will appear (see Figure 2-34). In this dialog box you can select the new key signature and the parameters of how the new key signature will affect the score. You can also create nonstandard key signatures and specify whether you want any music currently in the score to be transposed to the new key signature.

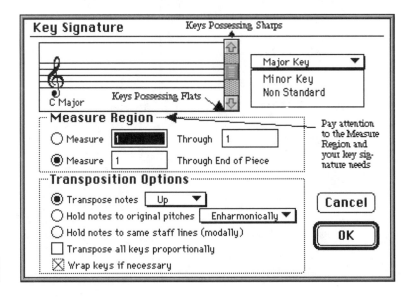

Figure 2-34

Always set up your first key signatures before you input note data so that you will not have to correct transposition problems later.

2-H Editing the Key Signature

This drill will show you how to change the key for the whole piece.

1. Scroll back to measure 1.

2. Click the Key Signature Tool . A handle will appear on every barline.

3. Click the first measure within the staff lines. A dialog box will appear.

4. With this particular dialog box, use the scroll bar to select a new key. Click the up arrow to add sharps or subtract flats from the key signature. Click the down arrow to add flats or subtract sharps.

5. Click the up arrow on the scroll bar once, so that one sharp appears.

6. At the bottom of the dialog box Finale lets you specify whether or not you want to transpose the notes when you change the key signature. Leave the settings as they are; you are transposing the song up to G.

7. Now specify what region of measures you want to be affected by the new key. Not the first radio button, from Measure X to Measure X for a specific measure range, but the second option, from the selected measure to the end of the piece.

   ⦿ Measure [1]   Through End of Piece

8. Click OK (or press the Return key). The dialog box goes away, and your piece is instantly transposed to the key of G.

Metatools

Metatools are one-keystroke equivalents for creating score changes—especially useful if you need to insert many changes in key signatures, meter changes, articulations, chord symbols, musical expressions, or repeats into your score. The number keys (0 through 9) and letters (A through Z) can be individually assigned a different Metatool function. They are retained in your score until you change them. You can have different Metatool functions assigned for the Main Tool Palette tools that allow these Metatool assignments. Always keep in mind that you can program a Metatool to accomplish a task you perform often, thereby saving a considerable amount of time and repetition. When you save your document, you will also save your Metatool programming. Next time you open the document, you will have the same Metatools available to use or reprogram.

Most tools let you create up to 36 *macros* (an assignable function to the keys 0 through 9 and A through Z on the alphanumeric keyboard, called Metatools in Finale). These macros provide single-click access to an editing feature or symbol placement that might otherwise require interaction with a number of dialog boxes.

You can create Key Signature Metatools if you have to input many different key signatures or if you have created complex nonstandard key signatures.

To gain speed in creating scores, it is critically important to understand and use Metatools right from the beginning.

2-I Programming a Key Signature Metatool

1. Click the Key Signature Tool.

2. Press Shift and a single number key (0 through 9) or (A-Z).

3. Finale displays the Key Signature dialog box; choose the key signature you want to correspond to the number you pressed.

4. Click OK (or press the Enter or Return key).

5. When you program a Metatool for the Articulation Tool and Staff or Score Expressions, you will see a new number in parentheses to illustrate the alphanumeric key it is assigned to.

It is helpful to create a brief journal listing any Metatools you create in a score, especially if you will be returning to a score at a later time. When you save your file you also save any programmed Metatools.

2-J Using a Key Signature Metatool

1. Click the Key Signature Tool.

2. While pressing the number corresponding to the Metatool you programmed, click a measure.

3. Finale displays the Key Signature dialog box again (with the actual key signature already selected).

4. Specify the range of measures you want to affect, and whether or not you want existing music to be transposed.

Earlier versions of Finale only allowed number keys 1–8 to be assigned a function. Also, the option key was previously used to program a Metatool function.

The Time Signature Tool

In time signatures, the top number indicates the number of beats within each measure. The bottom number indicates the unit of time, or note value, that receives one beat. Though the upper figure is commonly termed the *numerator* and the lower the *denominator*, make sure that you do not consider a time signature a fraction.

Setting the Time Signature

When you click the **Time Signature Tool** 🎼, a handle appears on every barline of the piece. Click in a measure or on its handle where you want to insert a meter change; this will bring up the Time Signature dialog box, and you can select or create a new meter.

The Time Signature Tool allows you to select and create:

Standard meters

Nonstandard meters—compound and fractional meters can be expressed with automatic beaming—a function of defining the non-standard meter

Changing the Time Signature

When you click the Time Signature Tool **4** and click in any measure, you can change the time signature for your score. If you click on the clef or key signature area, nothing will happen; but if you click the middle of the measure (within the staff lines), the Time Signature dialog box appears (Figure 2-35).

There are two scroll bars in this box: the upper one controls the top number (numerator) of the time signature, and the bottom one controls the bottom number (denominator).

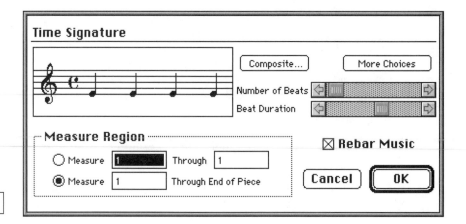

Figure 2-35

Use the upper scroll bar to change the upper number, which governs beats per measure.

If you click the lower scroll bar arrows, you set the rhythmic pulse—the lower number in the time signature. By changing the lower number from 4 to 8 (left arrow), you would decrease the value from a quarter note to an eighth note.

- Change the time signature in the score to 6/8 time. Click OK (or press the Enter or Return key).

- Choose Save from the File menu. Title your song; as you type, your title will appear in the text box in the "Save Finale File As" dialog box.

Always pay attention to the Measure Region in the Time Signature dialog box (see Figure 2-36[A]); the Measure Field

○ Measure [   ] Through [1   ]   should be used to change the time signature for a brief period of time in the score.

The default option of ● Measure [1   ] Through End of Piece   will change the time signature for the selected staff for the entire score.

If you do not get the expected results with the Time Signature Tool, check the setting in the Measure Region.

Measure Region

○ Measure [1   ] Through [1   ]

● Measure [1   ] Through End of Piece

Figure 2-36 (A)

Working with Complex and Composite Time Signatures

Finale allows you to create complex time signatures such as 5/8, 7/8, or 9/4 with ease. You can simply select the time signature numerator as needed and the denominator at the desired note duration. One important aspect of the time signature tool is the effect it has on the beaming of the notes in your score.

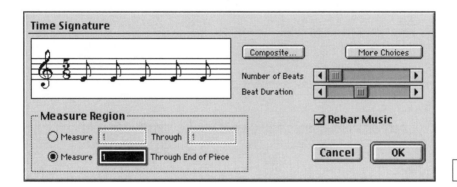

Figure 2-36 (B)

Notice how the 5/8 time signature does not beam any of the eight notes in Figure 2-36(C). To automatically control beaming, you must create a **Composite Time Signature.**

Figure 2-36 (C)

Since 5/8 can be grouped as 3 + 2 eight notes, setting up a composite time signature is accomplished by selecting the Composite button in the time signature dialog box. You simply need to add the beat groups to the top field (3+2) and specify the beat duration in the bottom field as in Figure 2-36(D). The composite time signature will now beam the notes as directed as in Figure 2-36(E).

Although Composite time signature notation is fine for a 20th century score, there may be times when you need just the time signature 5/8, not

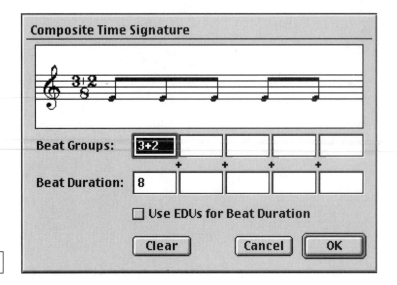

Figure 2-36 (D)

Figure 2-36 (E)

3+2/8, but want a specific beaming pattern. Select the More Choices button, and select the Use a Different Time Signature for Display option in Figure 2-36(F).

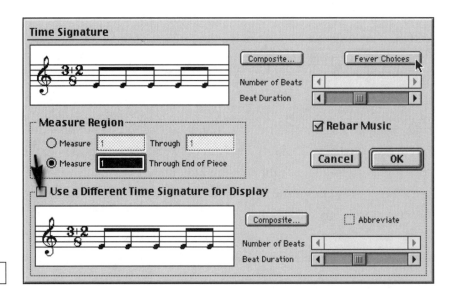

Figure 2-36 (F)

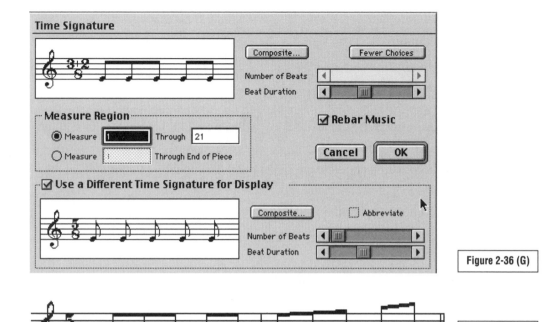

Figure 2-36 (G)

Figure 2-36 (H)

Use the sliders to set the time signature to display at the desired 5/8 and OK your choices. Now you are using a composite time signature 3+2/5 while the displayed time signature is 5/8. This setting will control your beaming when entering notes or update any notes you have placed in the score such as in Figure 2-36(H).

Programming a Time Signature Metatool

Click the Time Signature Tool. Press Shift and a key (0 through 9) or (A through Z). Finale displays the Time Signature dialog box; choose the time signature you want to correspond to the number you pressed. Click OK.

Using a Time Signature Metatool

When you click the Time Signature Tool, you can use the Shift key and an alphanumerical key (0-9 or A-Z) to program user-defined Metatool time signature changes. After programming time signature Metatools, press the number corresponding to the Metatool time signature change, and click a measure. Finale displays the Time Signature dialog box again (with the actual time signature already preprogrammed), so that you can specify the range of measures you want to affect.

The Measure Tool

When you click the **Measure Tool** 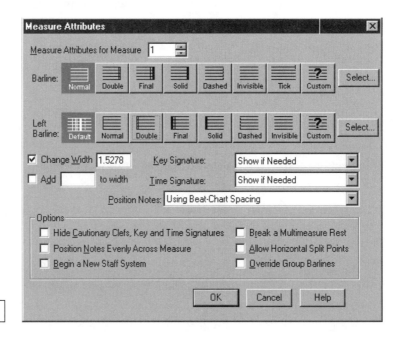, a handle appears on every barline; drag a barline's handle (or drag within the measure) to make the measure wider or narrower. If you are in Page View, the measure to the right of the barline will become narrower or wider to compensate. You can also double-click a measure (or its handle) to display the Measure Attributes dialog box, where you can specify a number of measure-specific parameters (Figure 2-37):

The barline type—double, final, solid, dashed, invisible (for free time or Gregorian chant notation) and tick (for film scores)

Whether to hide cautionary clefs, key and time signatures in your score if needed

Whether or not you want the key or time signature to appear in a measure

With Finale 2000 you can also specify left Barline attributes.

Figure 2-37

The Zoom Tool

The **Zoom Tool** is used to enlarge or reduce the music as it is displayed on the screen. You are not actually enlarging or reducing the printed size of the music—simply "zooming in" or "zooming out" the view as needed.

If the Zoom Tool is selected and you click (in Scroll View) or drag across the music (in Page View), Finale enlarges the display for detailed work. If you press Option/Ctrl-click while clicking or dragging, however, Finale makes the music smaller, to show more of the score on the screen. The plus sign in the magnifying glass will turn into a minus sign ⊖.

Special Mouse Clicks with the Zoom Tool:

Click the music to display it at twice its previous size.

Option-click the music to display it at half its previous size.

In the Windows version of Finale, the Zoom Tool is located in the Main Tool Bar.

In Page View, drag diagonally across a region of music to enlarge it just enough to fill your screen.

While using any other tool, ⌘-shift-click the screen to zoom in, even though the Zoom Tool is not selected. You can ⌘-option-shift-click to zoom out.

• Try the Zoom Tool keyboard shortcuts listed above.

The Hand Grabber Tool

With the **Hand Grabber Tool** selected, you can drag the mouse across the music in any direction to shift its position on your screen, as though you're sliding the score paper across your desk.

While using any other tool, press ⌘-option (not available in Windows) to switch temporarily to the Hand Grabber, so that you can make a display adjustment without having to move the mouse to the tool palette.

• Try the above Hand Grabber keyboard shortcut.

In most cases, the Hand Grabber Tool is a faster, more efficient way of moving around the score than using the scroll bars.

Chapter Two Review

Using the tools covered so far, you should now be able to: manipulate your Finale score by using these tools in the Finale Main Tool palette:

Program Metatools for determined tools.

Chapter Two Projects

1. Create a separate document for each of the following sections of this project: 2-1A, 2-1B, 2-1C, 2-1D, and place the proper brace or bracket preceding the instrumental or vocal staves.

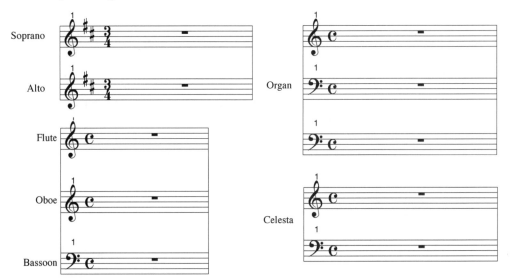

Hints:

See page 51, the Add Group and Bracket command.

Use the Staff Attributes dialog box to turn off staff names in the Items to Display area.

Drag the remaining staff name handle where desired.

2. Open a new document and save as "Project 2-2." Create the following score with multiple time signatures. Create a Metatool for each time signature change.

    Hints:

    Use the Measure Tool to create additional measures and to change measure size and add the final barline.

3. Create a new document as shown below and save as "Project 2-3."

    Hints:

    Use the Measure Tool to create additional measures, and to change measure size.

4. Create a new document as shown below and save as "Project 2-4." Create a Metatool for each key signature change.

    Hints:

    Turn off the display rests in the Staff Attributes dialog box.

    Use the Measure Tool to create additional measures.

    Use the Measure Tool to change measure size and add the final barline.

5. Symphonic Score:

Open a new document and use the Setup Wizard to create this symphonic score. Save As Project 2-5.

CHAPTER THREE

Simple Entry

Properly written, a musical note indicates without question two aspects of a musical sound. It is first a symbol indicating—by its position on the staff and by the clef used—a definite pitch to be played or sung. Second, it establishes—by the exact appearance of its three integral parts (Notehead, Stem, Flag)—the relative time duration of this musical sound.

—From *Music Notation* by Gardner Read, p. 63

Finale offers multiple methods for entering music: Simple Entry, Speedy Entry, Hyperscribe, Transcription Tool, and Standard MIDI File Conversion. We will begin with Simple Entry, which is easy to learn and does not require a MIDI keyboard.

Creating a Single Staff Score

- Open a new document and set up the key signature and time signature for the following Simple Entry input.

- Use the Measure Tool ![measure tool icon] to add seven more measures.

- Use the Key Signature Tool ![key signature tool icon] to select D major, as in Figure 3-1.

Figure 3-1

- Select the **Measure Attributes Tool** [■] and double-click the last measure to create a final double barline at the end of the score. [≣]

- Save as "Bill Bailey Excerpt"; we will come back to this file later in the book.

Entering Notes

To enter notes, click the **Simple Entry Tool** [♪] and two floating palettes will appear on the screen. In these palettes you will select the duration of a note or rest and other symbols for input in the score. Like the Main Tool Palette, you can move, dock, resize, hide, or reshape these palettes (see Figure 3-2).

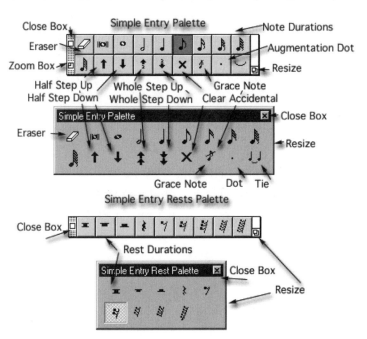

Figure 3-2

If the Simple Entry Palettes are not on the screen, you can select the Simple Entry Palette and simple rests pallette commands in the main Window menu.

3-A Placing Notes in a Score

1. To place notes in a score, open the "Bill Bailey Excerpt" document if you have closed it.

2. Click the **Quarter Note** icon [♩], and it will become highlighted.

3. Move the cursor to the first measure. As you drag the cursor above and below the staff, Finale draws temporary ledger lines to help you place new notes (see Figure 3-3).

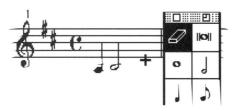

Figure 3-3 (Bill Bailey Excerpt)

Be careful that the ledger lines you are viewing attach to the staff in which you wish to place an entry.

4. Click the A note line anywhere below the first measure. A quarter note will appear.

5. Click the **Half Note** icon in the palette.

6. Click the B space just to the right of the first note. A half note will appear. Both notes are automatically adjusted for proper spacing.

7. Click on the Quarter Note icon again and add a D note to complete the first measure.

8. Save this file with the title "Bill Bailey Excerpt," since we will need to come back to it later in this chapter.

Erasing Notes

If you ever make a mistake, there is an Eraser [image] at the upper left of this tool palette. Select it, then position the cursor on any note you want to remove. A single click on the notehead turns it into a rest of the same value, and a double-click removes the note completely. A single click above or below the note also removes the note completely.

Accidentals

Since the last note you used was a quarter note, you do not have to change rhythmic values. Place three quarter note F#s in the second measure and use the **Half Step Down Tool** [↓] to click on the second F#. This will lower it by a half step to an F♮. This tool only affects one note at a time; therefore, the third F will retain the F# of the key signature.

If accidentals collide with barlines or key signatures in the score, first try the Redraw Screen command or the shortcut ⌘-**D**/Ctrl+D to correct this condition.

Scrolling

If you cannot see measure 3, click in the gray area to the right of the white box in the horizontal scroll bar. If you click to the right of the scroll box (the white square box), Finale moves your view of the music to the right; if you click to the left, your view shifts to the left. Remember that you can also advance one measure at a time by clicking the right and left arrows.

Dotted and Tied Notes

Continue entering notes up to measure 7 with the proper note duration tool using the example in Figure 3-4(A). At measure 7 place the A with the

Figure 3-4(A)

Quarter Note Tool and the C with the Half Note Tool. After inputting the C, select the **Dot Tool** ⎡ · ⎤ and click on the C's notehead to add the dot. Select the **Whole Note Tool** and insert the final C. After the final C is in the score, select the **Tie Tool** ⎡ ⌣ ⎤ and click on the dotted half note C's notehead. Finale will automatically add the tie. To delete a tie, select the Tie Tool and click on the first note of the tie.

Editing the Score

Finale 2000 has a great new feature that automatically respaces music as you enter it into the score. This is important because traditional notation uses different measure sizes that correspond to the amount of notes in the measure. The more notes, the more space allotted to that measure to make reading music easier. For example, a measure containing only a whole note will take up less space in the score than a measure that has eight eighth notes. When the **Automatic Music Spacing** option is selected, Finale will automatically adjust your music input. To turn this feature on, select Automatic Music Spacing (Figure 3-4 [B]) from Edit in the main menu.

Figure 3-4(B)

Note-Spacing Correction

After inputting notes, you may find that notes and/or accidentals will collide with barlines, key signatures, or other notes. This is because original insertion with the Simple Entry Tool spaces notes according to spacing equal to their time value. To correct this, do the following:

Selecting an Area for Editing

- Open the Finale file "Bill Bailey Excerpt" if not presently open.

- Click the Mass Mover Tool.

- Click just to the left of the staff. This will select an entire staff, and the entire line will be highlighted (see Figure 3-4 [C]).

Figure 3-4(C)

Click here to select all measures in a staff

If you click in a measure, you will select only that measure (see Figure 3-5 [A]).

Figure 3-5(A)

Click in a single measure to select it with the Mass Mover Tool

You can also click and drag to select multiple measures that you see on the screen.

If you hold down the Shift key, you can select a range of measures between the first and last selected measure. This will work when you click to select the first measure, then scroll and shift click a measure that is farther into the score and not presently on the screen, either forwards or backwards. The next section will explain how to correct collisions and spacing problems in a score.

Another great option with Finale is that you can select partial measures. This will allow you to transpose just a portion of a measure or apply a unique style to partial measures. To activate this feature you need to go to the Edit pull-down menu in the main menu and select the Select Partial Measures command (see Figure 3-5[B]). If you select this command again, you will turn this function off, and only complete measures are selectable.

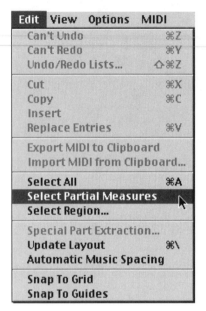

Figure 3-5(B)

Figure 3-5 (C) shows a partially selected measure. You can hold down the shift key to select more notes in a measure.

Figure 3-5(C)

With Finale 2000 you can apply a Staff Style to a partial measure for a mix and match look that is very effective, especially when working with jazz scores (see Figure 3-5 [D]).

Figure 3-5(D)

Music Spacing and Notes

Music Spacing commands are required to give your music a professional look. When music is first entered into Finale, each note is placed in a measure according to linear spacing. With linear spacing, a whole note takes up exactly twice the space of a half note, a half note takes up exactly twice the measure space of a quarter note, and so on. Linear spacing is a sensible way for Finale to initially deal with notes as they are entered into a score.

On the other hand, published music utilizes nonlinear spacing, where a whole note does not get as much horizontal space as four quarter notes, and two half notes take up less space than four quarter notes. With nonlinear spacing, smaller note durations take up more space, making them easier to read. Study the difference between linear- and nonlinear-spaced music in Figure 3-5 (E).

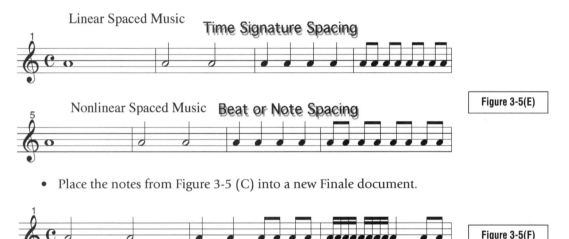

Figure 3-5(E)

- Place the notes from Figure 3-5 (C) into a new Finale document.

Figure 3-5(F)

- Once you have completed entering these notes into your score, select the Mass Mover Tool and highlight all the measures. Select Mass Edit from the main menu and the pull-down menu in Figure 3-5 (G) will appear. Move the cursor down to the **Music Spacing** command and select **Apply Beat Spacing**.

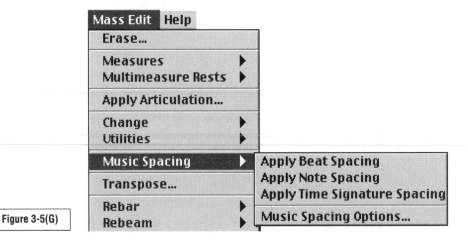

Figure 3-5(G)

Your score is now nonlinearly spaced, as in Figure 3-5 (H).

Figure 3-5(H)

Notice the expansion of the space between the sixteenth notes to make them easier to read. Beat Spacing has an additional advantage; you can manually adjust notes placed in the score up to the resolution of a single beat (beats are specified by the bottom note of a time signature).

- Select the Measure Tool 🔲. Notice that each measure now contains additional lower handles (see Figure 3-5 [I]).

Figure 3-5(I)

- Select the third measure's lower handle. This brings up a handle for each beat of the measure. By dragging these beat handles to the left or right you can easily respace the notes within a measure (see Figure 3-5 [J]).

Figure 3-5(J)

The second command, **Apply Note Spacing**, functions exactly the same as Apply Beat Spacing, but allows every note in a measure to have a handle for individual manual respacing (see Figure 3-5 [K]).

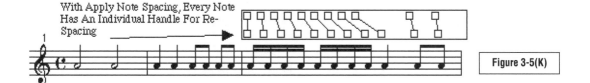

With Apply Note Spacing, Every Note Has An Individual Handle For Re-Spacing

Figure 3-5(K)

Erasing Excess Notes

Since Finale knows from the time signature how many notes should be in a measure, the problem shown in Figure 3-6 can happen if you make an input mistake. The solution is simple; use the Eraser Tool to delete the last note that would be possible in the measure, and the excess notes will slip out from under the next measure and become deletable.

Use The Eraser Tool Here

These notes are slipped under the second measure

Figure 3-6

Starting with version 3.7.2, there is a new Simple Entry command, **Check for Extra Notes**, in the main Finale menu. It should be a common practice to select this command so that you will not be able to input more notes in a measure than the time signature will allow (see Figures 3-7 and 3-8).

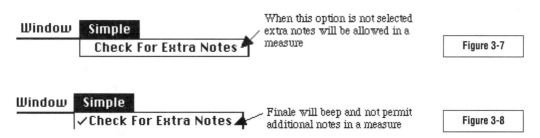

Window Simple
Check For Extra Notes

When this option is not selected extra notes will be allowed in a measure

Figure 3-7

Window Simple
✓**Check For Extra Notes**

Finale will beep and not permit additional notes in a measure

Figure 3-8

Numeric Pad Shortcuts

When using Simple Entry as a music-input method, you can simply hold down a number key on the Macintosh keypad/only numbers above on the QWERTY keyboard, and click the staff to assign the desired rhythm. Each number key corresponds to a rhythmic value, as seen in Figure 3-9; with this method all rhythm durations are available, rather than having to click one at a time in the palette. Hold down the Shift key and the number that corresponds to the desired rhythmic value key, and a rest of that value will be placed in your score.

Figure 3-9

Since the numeric pad shortcuts (if your laptop does not have a numeric pad, use the numbers in the alphanumeric keyboard) make the Simple Entry Palette tools inactive, select a tool other than note duration for multiple entry possibilities. After you analyze your score, select the Simple Entry tool that is most advantageous for your score activity.

For example, if there are numerous dotted notes in your score, select the Dot Tool [·] from the Simple Entry Palette. Place notes in the score with the numeric pad shortcuts, subsequently using the Simple Entry Palette's active Dot Tool to augment the necessary note durations with the numeric pad. Alternately, select the Tie Tool [⌣] if your score has many tied notes. Choose the correct tool for changing note input with the numeric pad shortcuts, such as the **Grace Note Tool** [♪], **Accidental Tool** [↓], or Eraser Tool [✐] for easy correction of mistakes.

Playing Back the Score

- Select the **Playback Controls** command in the Finale Window menu. A Transport Control window will appear with button functions comparable to a cassette recorder's transport controls (see Figure 3-10).

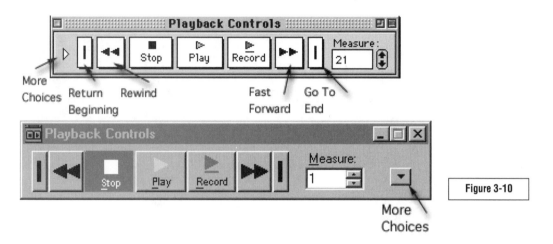

Figure 3-10

- Click the **Play** button [▶ Play]; playback begins from the first measure.

- Click the **Rewind** button [◀◀] to move back one measure; hold the mouse button down to rapidly move back measures until the beginning of the score is arrived at. Playback will start at whatever measure you release this button.

- Click the **Fast Forward** button [▶▶] to move ahead one measure; hold the mouse button down, and the score will rapidly move ahead by measures until the end of the score is reached. Playback will start at whatever measure you release this button.

- The **Return to Beginning** [I◀◀] and **Go to End** [▶▶I] buttons will immediately take you to the beginning or end of the score respectively.

- Click the **More Choices** button and the Playback window will expand. Figures 3-11 and 3-12(A) illustrate the extended Playback window options.

Additional Playback Controls

- Select the ▷ button from the Playback Controls dialog box. The dialog box expands, as shown in Figure 3-11. Select the Flyout ▽ if you want to reduce the size of the dialog box after adjusting your setting.

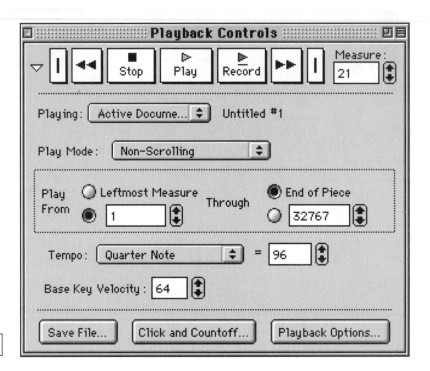

Figure 3-11

The Mac version of Finale 2000 can play your score without a synthesizer by using Quicktime Instruments when The Internal Speaker Playback Option is selected (see Figure 3-12[B]).

The Play Mode pop-up menu will allow the music to scroll to follow play (see Figure 3-13). This is a very valuable feature for checking your work and in educational situations where you are projecting a score for a class. A pointer will move along the top of the score, giving visual feedback of the notes, following the bouncing ball (see Figure 3-14). In Finale 2000, the pointer will also follow playback in the Page View.

Check the Finale 2000 Installation and Tutorials book for setting up a MIDI System (xi-xiii).

Active Document Will Playback The
Score Which You Presently Have Open

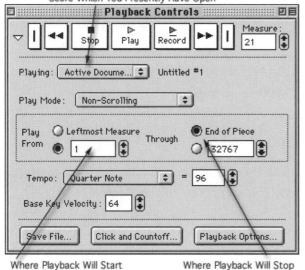

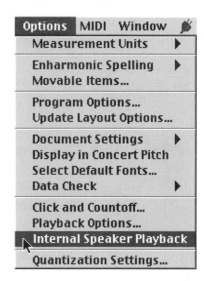

Where Playback Will Start   Where Playback Will Stop

Figure 3-12(A)

Figure 3-12(B)

Internal Speaker Playback is available for the Mac only.

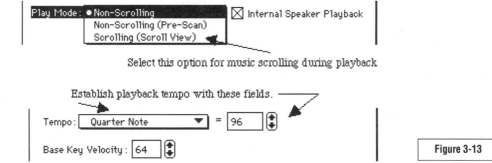

Select this option for music scrolling during playback

Establish playback tempo with these fields.

Figure 3-13

Moving Pointer that shows notes or chords
being played by Finale in Scrolling

[Staff 1]

Figure 3-14

- When you have completed this example, use computer playback to
  aurally check your notes and rhythm by clicking on Play in the Playback
  window.

Special Score Considerations

Notated rhythm serves the composer and the performer in two spheres: it exists not only for the ear alone, but also for the eye. The eye helps to clarify the rhythmic subtleties that the ear alone cannot distinguish.

—From *Music Notation* by Gardner Read, pp. 27-28

3-B Entering Triplets and Tuplets

1. Open a new document and set up the key signature and time signature for the following Simple Entry input example in Figure 3-15 (A).

2. Use the Measure Tool to add three more measures, and the Measure Attributes Tool to create a final barline at the end of measure 4.

Figure 3-15(A)

3. Place a half note and a quarter note at any pitch into measure 1. Select the Eraser Tool and click *on the noteheads for each*. The reason that the pitches are not critical is that these notes are used for rest durations, not pitch. Finale will automatically center and place the rests in the staff. Do not click above the notes with the Eraser Tool, because this will completely erase or delete that note.

4. Place the three D eighth notes in measure 2. Triplets are created with the **Tuplet Tool** .

5. Select it now. When you click on the first note of a series of notes with the Tuplet Tool, the Tuplet Definition dialog box will appear, as shown in Figure 3-15 (B).

6. On the left side of the screen there are various options for defining the triplet (tuplet). By using these buttons and boxes, you define the value

to be played, in the space of, and what note value. It is called the Tuplet Tool since a tuplet could be 5 in the time of 4, etc., not just triplets. For now, we want three eighths in the time of two eighths. Since you clicked on an eighth note, this value is already selected.

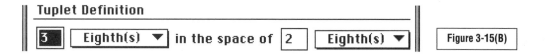

Figure 3-15(B)

7. In the lower left-hand side of the dialog box you can specify how the tuplet should look on the screen. Click on the "Number," "Shape," and "Placement" pop-up menus to define the visual appearance of the tuplet. The pop-up options are shown in Figures 3-16 (A) and (B). Then click OK, Enter, or the Return key.

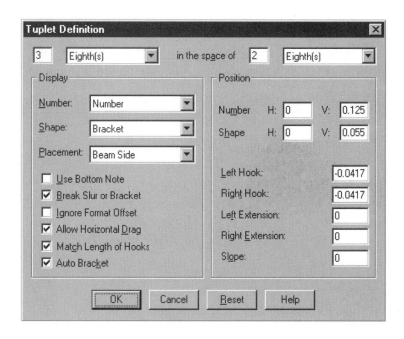

Figure 3-16(A)

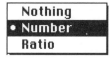

Figure 3-16(B)

Editing Triplets and Tuplets

If a bracket does not appear as desired, click on the first note of the triplet in the score, and handles will appear to adjust the tuplet's look. If you have selected the manual option in the placement pop-up menu, you can move a tuplet's handles in the following ways (Figure 3-17).

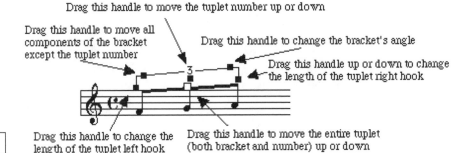

Drag this handle to move the tuplet number up or down

Drag this handle to move all components of the bracket except the tuplet number

Drag this handle to change the bracket's angle

Drag this handle up or down to change the length of the tuplet right hook

Figure 3-17

Drag this handle to change the length of the tuplet left hook

Drag this handle to move the entire tuplet (both bracket and number) up or down

8. Use the Dot Tool and Tie Tool to finish Drill 3-B. If you are creating a triplet at the end of a measure, you may have to slip the last note of the tuplet under the next measure. Then select the Tuplet Tool, and click on the first note of the tuplet. The last note will then slide into the proper measure.

3-C Tuplet and Music Spacing

1. Open a new document.

2. Insert the notes from Figure 3-18 (A) into your document.

Figure 3-18(A)

3. Select the Tuplet Tool and click on the first note of the quintuplet. When the Tuplet Definition dialog box appears, use the pop-up note value menus to select note value definitions for the tuplet. Figure 3-18 (B) illustrates the note duration option for **in the space of**. It is set incorrectly at 16th(s).

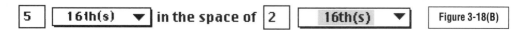
Figure 3-18(B)

4. Point and click in the second pop-up menu in the Tuplet Definition dialog box and set it to quarter(s) as in Figure 3-18 (C).

5. If the tuplets do not turn out correctly, click on the first note of a tuplet, select a handle, press the Delete key, and start again.

| Half(s) |
| Dotted Quarter(s) |
| • Quarter(s) |
| Dotted Eighth(s) |
| Eighth(s) |
| Dotted 16th(s) |
| 16th(s) |
| Dotted 32nd(s) |
| 32nd(s) |
| 64th(s) |

Figure 3-18(C)

6. Place the remaining note values into measure 1.

7. Use the Measure Tool to add two more measures, and the Measure Attributes Tool to create a final barline at the end of measure 3. Then complete input of measures 2 and 3 with notes and tuplets as in Figure 3-18 (D). Finally, apply either Beat or Note Spacing.

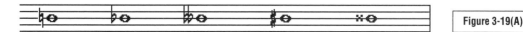
Figure 3-18(D)

Accidentals

In theory, any notated pitch or scale degree can have five different permutations. The original unaltered note on a line or a space; a lowered or doubly lowered note; and finally, a raised or doubly raised note (see Figure 3-19[A]).

Figure 3-19(A)

In practice, scale degrees are not subjected to all five variants, but any tone can be both lowered or raised, with some being doubly lowered or raised. To achieve these simple alterations, signs must be placed before the note to designate changes in sounding pitch. These signs are called *accidentals:*

The natural ♮

The flat ♭

The sharp ♯

The double flat 𝄫

The double sharp 𝄪

The general principles governing accidentals (independent of key signatures) are as follows (see Figure 3-19 [B]):

1. To lower a natural scale-degree, use a flat.

2. To lower a flatted degree, use a double flat.

3. *To raise a double flat, use a natural followed by a single flat.

4. To raise a flatted degree, use a natural.

5. To raise a natural degree, use a sharp.

6. To raise a sharped degree, use a double sharp.

7. *To lower a double sharp, use a natural followed by a single sharp.

8. To lower a sharped degree, use a natural.

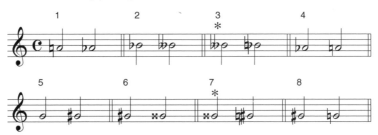

Figure 3-19(B)

Although there are double flats and double sharps, there is no such thing as a double natural. Triple flats and sharps are likewise meaningless, as they would only duplicate the single flat or sharp on the next adjacent note.

—From *Music Notation* by Gardner Read, pp. 125-126

---

*General principles 3 and 7 cannot be created with the Simple Entry Tool and are beyond the scope of this book.

THE FINALE PRIMER

Accidental Tools

↑ Half Step Up Tool—raises a note one half step.

↓ Half Step Down Tool—lowers a note one half step.

↑ Whole Step Up Tool—raises a note one whole step up.

↓ Whole Step Down Tool—lowers a note one whole step down.

✕ Remove Accidental Tool— click on a notehead with any accidental, and it will be removed.

3-D Using the Accidental Tools

1. Create the musical example in Figure 3-20 using the Simple Entry Accidental Tools.

Figure 3-20

2. Use the Measure and Key Signature Tools first. Then input notes and add the accidentals one measure at a time.

3. If you make a mistake, you can use the **Remove Accidental Tool** ✕ to clear an inappropriate accidental.

The Grace Note

Grace notes are literal reductions of full-sized note-forms, without actual rhythmic value in a measure, as the time in which they are to be performed must be subtracted from an adjacent beat. If unaccented—their most familiar guise—they exist by the "grace" of the beat preceding. If accented they exist by the "grace" of the beat following.

—From *Music Notation*, p. 238

3-E Creating Grace Notes

1. Open a new document, create a 12/8 time signature, and use the Measure Tool to add one more measure. Input the notes in measure 1 of Figure 3-21.

2. Hold the Shift key and the number 5 key in the numeric keypad down, and click at the beginning of measure 1. This will place a rest in the score without having to use the Eraser Tool to convert the entered place-keeper note.

3. Use the Simple Entry Tool Palette and keyboard shortcuts to place the notes.

4. Use the Simple Entry keyboard shortcuts to place the value of the grace note.

5. Select the **Grace Note Tool** [♪] and click on the regular notehead that you wish to convert into a grace note. Enter the additional regular notes with keyboard shortcuts.

6. Use the Measure Tool to placed the double barline in the last measure.

Entering Chords

To create a chord, simply select the duration and click in the same area, either under or above the notehead, to add chord tones (see Figure 3-22).

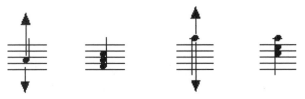

Figure 3-22

Add chord tones by clicking under or above the first entered pitch of the desired chord

The order in which you enter notes does not matter

Tied Notes

Ties are inputted by selecting the Tie Tool ⌣, and clicking on the first note of the tie. Each note in a chord may or may not contain a tie, but if all chord tones have a tie, you must click on all the noteheads in the chord.

Ties have improved but are somewhat problematic in Finale, as they sometimes are hard to see when a barline hides part of a tie, or the tied notes are very close together. To correct a tie problem, use the **Special Tools** and the Tie Tool from the Special Tool Palette and click on the first note of a tie. Click in the tie's center handle (Figure 3-23), and use the arrow keys to reposition the tie.

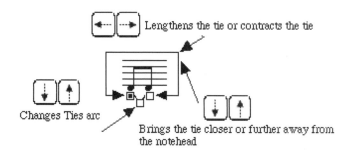

Figure 3-23

Smart Shapes

- Click on the **Smart Shape Tool** . A new floating palette appears, containing icons for slurs, crescendos, *8va* markings, and several kinds of brackets and lines.

This floating palette is similar to others you have encountered; you move it by dragging its drag bar, and change its shape or size by dragging its size box in the lower-right corner.

Each tool selection in this palette will contain a description of how it works in the message bar (see Figure 3-24).

The curves and lines of this palette are called Smart Shapes, because they behave intelligently:

If the measure widens, so does the Smart Shape attached to it

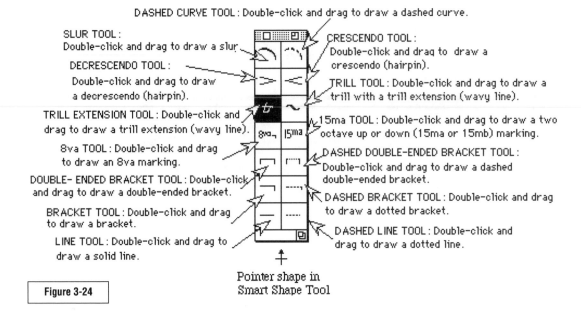

DASHED CURVE TOOL : Double-click and drag to draw a dashed curve.

SLUR TOOL :
Double-click and drag to draw a slur.

DECRESCENDO TOOL :
Double-click and drag to draw
a decrescendo (hairpin).

TRILL EXTENSION TOOL : Double-click and
drag to draw a trill extension (wavy line).

8va TOOL : Double-click and drag
to draw an 8va marking.

DOUBLE- ENDED BRACKET TOOL : Double-click
and drag to draw a double-ended bracket.

BRACKET TOOL : Double-click and drag
to draw a bracket.

LINE TOOL : Double-click and drag to
draw a solid line.

CRESCENDO TOOL :
Double-click and drag to draw a
crescendo (hairpin).

TRILL TOOL : Double-click and drag to draw a
trill with a trill extension (wavy line).

15ma TOOL : Double-click and drag to draw a two
octave up or down (15ma or 15mb) marking.

DASHED DOUBLE-ENDED BRACKET TOOL :
Double-click and drag to draw a dashed
double-ended bracket.

DASHED BRACKET TOOL : Double-click and drag
to draw a dotted bracket.

DASHED LINE TOOL : Double-click and
drag to draw a dotted line.

Pointer shape in
Smart Shape Tool

Figure 3-24

If a Smart Shape begins at the end of one line of music and continues onto the next, it automatically breaks in two.

Entering a Smart Shape

- Select the **Slur Tool** icon if is not presently selected.

- Position the cursor just under the first grace note of the melody from Figure 3-21. The cursor, you will notice, has an up arrow, which points to the staff to which the Smart Shape will be attached.

- Double-click the mouse, but hold the button down after the second click. Drag the mouse to the right, to the end of the second measure. You have just drawn a phrase marking. As long as you hold the button down, you can continue moving the endpoint of the phrase marking.

- To create a Smart Shape phrase marking, double-click where you want it to begin.

- Without releasing the mouse button, drag to the right.

- Release the mouse button when the right endpoint of the phrase marking is where you want it.

- Release the mouse. Take a look. Is the phrase marking exactly where you want it? Does it arc too high or too low?

Editing a Smart Shape

A Smart Shape is easy to edit. When surrounded by a rectangle, it is currently selected (see Figure 3-25 [A]).

Figure 3-25(A)

A shaping handle appears for Line, Curve, or Slur Tool shapes. For even more control, you can make "control" handles appear on Curve, Slur, or Bracket Tool shapes by double-clicking in or on a selected shape.

The Smart Shape editing rectangle shown in Figure 3-25 (B) can be manipulated in the following four ways:

Dotted outline shows that the placed Smart Shape can be edited

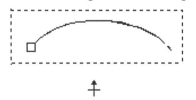

Figure 3-25(B)

1. Dragging the right end of the rectangle stretches the phrase marking's endpoint further right.

2. Dragging the left end of the rectangle stretches the phrase marking's endpoint further left.

3. Dragging the outer middle section changes the arc (or the width of a crescendo's opening).

4. Dragging the inner middle section moves the entire shape.

If you do any of this dragging while pressing the Shift key, you can constrain your cursor to perfect horizontal or vertical movements. If you drag the outer middle section of a slur or phrase marking while pressing the Option key, you can create an asymmetrical arc instead of the usual perfect arc.

Click outside a Smart Shape to deselect it. Its handles disappear. Keep in mind that:

> The arrow keys nudge a selected object by 1/288th of an inch or one screen pixel on the score.

> The Shift key constrains the cursor to vertical or horizontal movements only.

- Experiment with adding phrase marks above the melody with the Smart Shape Tool.

- Position the cursor below the first melody note in measure 1. Double-click and drag to the end of the measure. The new phrase marking displays the reshaping rectangle, letting you know that it's selected. The first one you drew, meanwhile, is no longer selected. Instead, it displays a small square handle. To select a Smart Shape that does not display its reshaping rectangle, click its handle.

- Feel free to experiment with these Smart Shapes. Decrease the depth of the second phrase marking you created. Try adding a crescendo or decrescendo.

- If you want to flip a Smart Shape, select it and go to The Smart Shape Menu and select Direction then Flip. (see Figure 3-25[C]).

Deleting a Smart Shape

To delete a Smart Shape, click the handle to select the shape and press the Delete key. Every type of Smart Shape displays a small square handle on the screen (unless it's already been selected, in which case it has a reshaping rectangle).

3-F Creating a Single Line Nonpitched Rhythm Study

This drill will teach you how to create a nonpitched rhythm study.

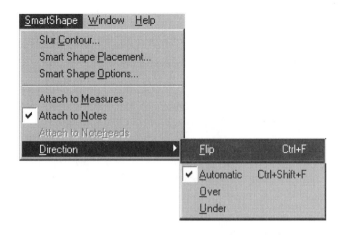

Figure 3-25(C)

1. Create a new document with three empty measures. This exercise will use a 4/4 time signature instead of the common time abbreviation.

2. Select Options from the main menu and select the **Document Settings** command. From its submenu select **Time Signature Options** (see Figure 3-26 [A]).

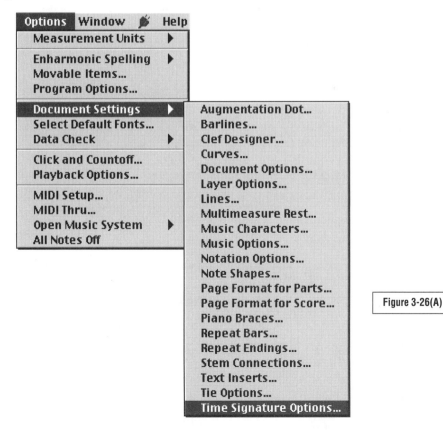

Figure 3-26(A)

3. When the Time Signature Options dialog box appears, deselect the Abbreviate Common Time To box (see Figure 3-26 [B]) and your score will now contain a nonabbreviated 4/4 time signature.

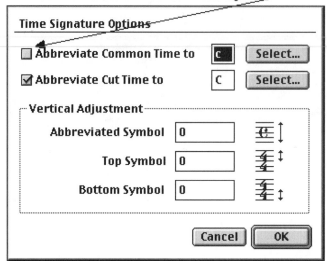

Figure 3-26(B)

4. Enter all the notes at one pitch in a five-line staff on a single line (see Figure 3-26 [C]).

Figure 3-26(C)

5. Select the Staff Tool's pull-down Staff menu and go to the Edit Staff Attributes command. Adjust the Staff Line Number pull-down menu in the Staff Attributes dialog box to either of the two single-line options (see Figure 3-26 [D]).

Figure 3-26(D)

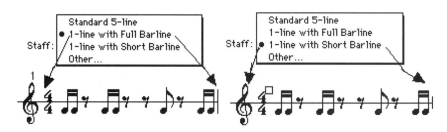

6. The notes in Figure 3-26 (D) were entered on the pitch of A in the five-line staff. If you have entered different pitches, the noteheads will be at different levels when a one-line staff is created.

7. To create a rhythm study, enter the rhythms at a single pitch so they will not be stepped as in Figure 3-27.

Figure 3-27

Alternate Meter and Note Beaming

Changing meter and note beaming is easily accomplished.

• Create the example in Figure 3-28.

Figure 3-28

• Select the Time Signature Tool and double-click in the first measure. This brings up the Time Signature Tool dialog box (see Figure 3-29).

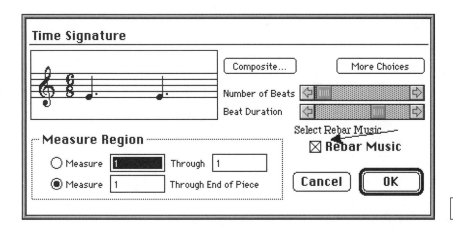

Figure 3-29

• By adjusting the Beat Duration scroll bar and the Number of Beats scroll bar you can create a 6/8 time signature that will beam the music in the desired fashion. The two dotted quarter notes mean that all the music in the measure range you select will be rebeamed, as in Figure 3-30.

Figure 3-30

Since Finale automatically beams the notes by time signatures, you can change the beaming pattern at any time.

Alternate Notation

You can create alternate notation (one-bar repeats, two-bar repeats, slash notation, blank notation, and normal notation) by using the Staff Tool, in the Main Tool Palette.

For All Staff Measures In a Score

Click the Staff Tool, and select Edit Staff Attributes or Edit Staff Styles from the Staff menu, or double-click a measure in the score. The Staff Attributes dialog box in Figure 3-31(A) will appear.

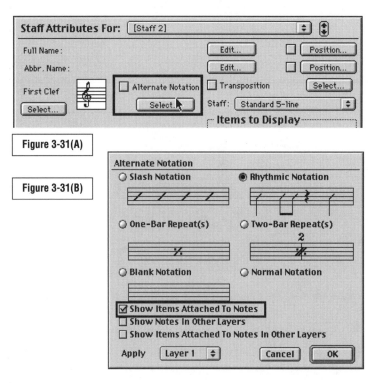

Figure 3-31(A)

Figure 3-31(B)

Click on the Select button underneath Alternate notation and the Alternate Notation dialog box appears on the screen (see Figure 3-31 [B]).

The upper portion of this dialog box selects the style of alternate notation, and in the lower portion the box next to Show Items Attached To Notes should always be checked. Make sure it is, since this will attach chord symbols you create to a staff's alternate notation.

This method will change all the measures in a staff to alternate notation. To change alternate notation to normal, use the same steps but select the Normal Notation radio button.

For Partial Staff Measures In a Score

Select the Staff Tool and select the measures or partial measure(s) to be converted. Go to the Staff menu and select the Apply Staff Styles Command as in Figure 3-31(C).

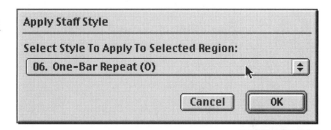

Figure 3-31 (C)

The Apply Staff Style dialog box in Figure 3-31(D) will appear. By simply choosing one of the styles from the Select Style To Apply To Selected Region fly-out, the desired alternate notation will take effect.

Notice in Figure 3-31(D) that the style 06 has a pre-assigned Meta Tool option (O). By simply highlighting measure(s) and touching the alphanumeric Meta Tool assignment (O), you can quickly and easily change to alternate notation.

Figure 3-31(D)

Meta Tool Pre-Assignments

(S) Slash Notation, (R) Rhythmic Notation, (M) Normal Notation, and (T) Two-Bar Repeat

If you do not see chord symbols when you add rhythmic alternate notation, make sure that the Show Items Attached To Notes is selected in the Alternate Notation dialog box, see Figure 3-31(B). With Finale 2000 you can easily have a partial measure in alternate notation and the rest in normal.

Figure 3-32

- Once you have selected Alternate Notation with the Mass Mover/Mass Edit options, use the Staff Attributes Tool to create a one-line staff to complete this example (Figure 3-33).

Figure 3-33

Creating an Anacrusis or Pickup Measure

The easiest method for creating a pickup measure is to enter the notes normally, and then make the measure narrower as necessary with the Measure Attributes Tool. But such a pickup measure will not play back correctly—the pickup will be played as though it falls at the start of the measure, and the rest of the measure will be heard as silence.

To create a pickup measure within a piece that does not disrupt playback in this way, follow the steps in Drill 3-G.

3-G Entering Pickup Notes

1. First, enter the pickup notes.

2. For the moment, notate them at the beginning of the measure, even though they will eventually be right-justified (see Figure 3-34 [A]).

Figure 3-34(A)

3. To input a cut time signature, select the Time Signature Tool, click in measure 1, and set the number of beats and beat durations exactly as shown in Figure 3-34 (B).

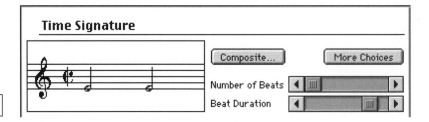

Figure 3-34(B)

4. Select the **Mirror Tool** 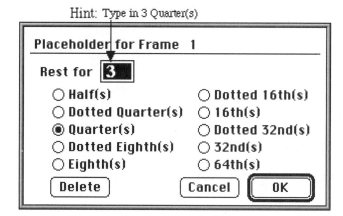, and click in the first measure. A "Rest For" box will appear (see Figure 3-35).

Hint: Type in 3 Quarter(s)

Placeholder for Frame 1

Rest for **3**

○ Half(s)   ○ Dotted 16th(s)
○ Dotted Quarter(s)   ○ 16th(s)
● Quarter(s)   ○ Dotted 32nd(s)
○ Dotted Eighth(s)   ○ 32nd(s)
○ Eighth(s)   ○ 64th(s)

(Delete)   (Cancel) (OK)

Figure 3-35

5. Specify the duration of the rest preceding the pickup notes (a "place-holder" value) by clicking the appropriate duration button (dotted note values are also available) and entering an appropriate number (3) in the "Rest for" text box.

6. Click OK or press Return. Another box will appear, asking whether the "placeholder" should be applied to this measure in this staff only, or all the staves of this measure (see Figure 3-36).

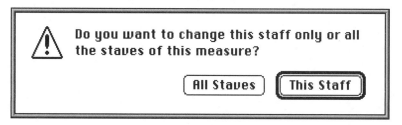

⚠ **Do you want to change this staff only or all the staves of this measure?**

(All Staves) (This Staff)

Figure 3-36

7. Click the appropriate choice.

8. Whenever the Mirror Tool is selected, any pickup measure that has been created with this tool will display the Mirror icon (see Figure 3-37).

Shows that there is a Mirror Tool placeholder in this measure

Figure 3-37

Respacing Pickup Notes

Finale must be told to create pickup or anacrusis notes in a measure. Notes are inserted into a score according to their natural placement as stated by the meter. This creates a wide blank space in the left part of the measure. If you use the following technique, you can eliminate the empty left portion of the anacrusis measure.

- Click the Mass Mover Tool ▦ and select the pickup measure. If you have multiple staves, select the one with the most notes.

- From the Music Spacing submenu of the Mass Edit menu, choose Apply Note Spacing. Finale respaces the measure.

An Alternate Method

- Click the Measure Attributes Tool ▤. A handle appears on each barline.

- Drag the top handle on the right barline of the pickup measure to decrease the measure width, if desired (see Figure 3-38).

Figure 3-38

Now, your finished score should look like Figure 3-39.

Figure 3-39

Chapter Three Review

Using the tools covered in Chapter Three, you now know how to input notes and manipulate your Finale scores. Make sure that you have mastered the following techniques:

Simple Entry and all power key shortcuts

Alteration of notes in the score using the following Simple Entry Tools: accidentals, augmentation dots, ties, and grace notes

Using the Mass Mover tool to respace notes in your score

Playback of your score

Using the Tuplet Tool to create triplets and tuplets

Using the Smart Shapes Tool for slurs, decrescendos, crescendos, trills and 8vas

Creating a single-line staff rhythm study

Creating alternate notation for Slash Notation, Bar Repeats, Blank Notation, and Normal Notation

Adding an anacrusis or pickup to your score

Chapter Three Projects

1. Create a separate document for each section of this project, Project 3-1A and Project 3-1B.

Hint:

The pitch B is already lowered; you need to lower it one more time.

2. Open a new document and save as "Project 3-2." Create the following score using Simple Entry techniques.

3. Open a new document and save as "Project 3-3." Create the following score using Simple Entry techniques. Pay close attention to the grace notes.

4. Open a new document and save as "Project 3-4." Create the following score using Simple Entry techniques. Pay close attention to clefs and the final barline.

5. Open a new document and save as "Project 3-5." Create the following score using Simple Entry techniques and alternate notation.

Hint: Use the Alternate Notation available with Staff Tool.

CHAPTER FOUR

Speedy Entry

Setting Up Speedy Entry

Speedy Entry, as the name implies, is a very quick and practical way to input score data. As mentioned in Chapter One, always use Scroll View when inputting note and score entries. Scroll View is much quicker than Page View, which takes time to calculate page layout and requires more screen redraws.

There are two important ways to enter music with the Speedy Entry Tool:

"Use MIDI":

Input music via a keyboard

Input music via another MIDI controller (wind, guitar, etc.)

"Type in" music:

Use the letter keys to specify the pitch of each note

Use the number keys to specify the rhythm of each note

- Click the **Speedy Entry Tool** . The Speedy menu option at the top right of the screen will control the manner in which this tool functions.
- Click and hold on the word Speedy so that the pull-down menu appears (see Figure 4-1).

Additional menu option once the Speedy Entry Tool is selected

| 🍎 | File | Edit | View | Options | Window | 🖊 | Speedy | Help |

It is necessary to play the correct pitches when entering with MIDI from a keyboard or MIDI controller; especially when in keys other than "C." You must play the actual pitch of the accidentals you want to appear in the score. Key signatures will not apply to MIDI input.

*The laminated Quick Reference Card that comes with Finale should always be close at hand when working with Speedy Entry. It has all the Speedy Entry keypad commands in one spot. (Quick Reference, page 8). This information is also available under the Speedy Main Menu command **Speedy** navigation.*

Figure 4-1

- Make sure that there is a check mark beside Use MIDI Keyboard. If you need to enter music without a synthesizer, you can enter music with the Speedy Entry Tool by turning off the Use MIDI Keyboard option and typing directly into the score (see Figure 4-2).

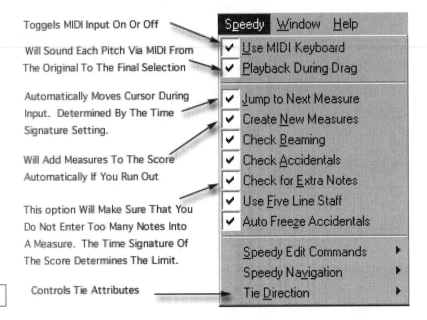

Toggels MIDI Input On Or Off

Will Sound Each Pitch Via MIDI From The Original To The Final Selection

Automatically Moves Cursor During Input. Determined By The Time Signature Setting.

Will Add Measures To The Score Automatically If You Run Out

This option Will Make Sure That You Do Not Enter Too Many Notes Into A Measure. The Time Signature Of The Score Determines The Limit.

Controls Tie Attributes

Figure 4-2

- It is a good idea to select the Check For Extra Notes command so that Finale will bring up a dialog box if you attempt to enter too many notes in a measure. This situation will sometimes occur when you do not have the **Jump To Next Measure** command checked. Each of the radio buttons in Figure 4-3 provides a different option for dealing with too many notes in a measure.

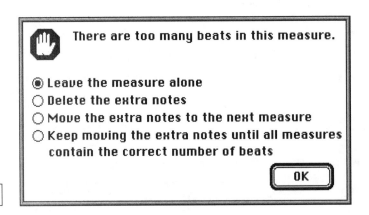

Figure 4-3

Note Input

- Click in the first measure of your space. The measure will now contain a rectangular frame similar to Figure 4-4, with a thin vertical cursor at the left side of it called the **insertion bar.** There is also a short horizontal cursor called the **pitch crossbar,** which indicates pitch.

- Use the up/down arrow keys to move the pitch crossbar, and the left/right arrow keys to move the insertion bar. Press the zero key to exit the frame. Press zero again to re-enter the frame.

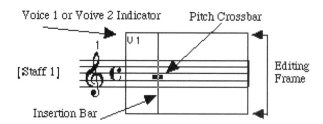

Figure 4-4

In the upper left-hand corner of the frame you will see a tiny "V1" telling you that you are ready to enter Voice 1. Multiple voices, such as stems up and stems down, are referred to in Finale as Voice 1 and Voice 2, respectively.

Testing for MIDI Signal

- Play middle C on your synthesizer.

- While holding down the synthesizer key, press the 4 key on your computer's alphanumeric keyboard. If your MIDI system is hooked up correctly, a middle C eighth note will appear. If your synthesizer is not transmitting correctly to the computer, you will see a quarter rest. In that case, consult the topic "MIDI" in the on-line documentation.

A good place to start with MIDI trouble-shooting is to make sure that the MIDI In and MIDI Out cables are wired correctly.

MIDI Input

Always play and hold the pitch first, then hit a numeric key. The synthesizer provides Finale with pitch information, while you provide rhythmic information by pressing the proper key.

By holding down a synthesizer key(s) when you press a numeric key, you get a single note or chord.

When you press a numeric key without a synthesizer key being held down, you get a rest.

- Hold down the D key on your synthesizer and press the 4 key again; then hold down E (press 4); then F (press 4). These notes will be automatically beamed, and you will have just built the first four notes of a C scale (see Figure 4-5).

Figure 4-5

Triplets

If you press Option and the number 3 key 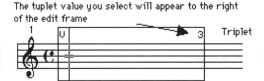/Ctrl+3, the following note values you enter will become triplets in the score (see Figure 4-6). Similarly, by pressing Option-5/Ctrl+5, you will input a quintuplet; Option-6/Ctrl+6, a sextuplet, etc. If you need to create a complex or compound triplet, use the Tuplet Tool.

Figure 4-6

The tuplet value you select will appear to the right of the edit frame

Correcting Mistakes

To correct a note entry mistake, move the insertion bar (by pressing the arrow keys or by clicking on a note) and then press the Delete key/Shift+(.). This will remove a note, rest, or chord from your score.

Moving from Measure to Measure

- Press the zero (0)/(0) key to exit the editing frame, or click on any blank part of the screen. The editing frame will disappear.

- Press the zero key again. This key also takes you back into the editing frame.

- Press the left bracket ([)/([) key on your keyboard. Finale moves you back to the first measure.

Remember to use the Update Layout display to confirm your score's true appearance.

The left and right bracket keys move the current editing frame one measure to the left or right, respectively.

Select Redraw Screen from the View menu, or press ⌘-**D**/Ctrl+D. Then press the zero key again to re-enter the Speedy editing frame.

When you press the ⬅ and ➡ keys on the keyboard, the insertion bar will move in the direction indicated by one note or rest. You can also move the insertion bar by clicking on any note with the mouse.

Editing with the Speedy Entry Keypad

Changing a Note's Duration

- Position the insertion bar on the first note from the example in Figure 4-5 (middle C) and press the 5 key. In Speedy Entry, 5 means a quarter note duration, so your middle C eighth note will change to a quarter note. If you have entered an incorrect rhythm, line up the insertion bar with the note to be changed and press the appropriate key number for the desired duration.

- Press the 5 key three more times. You will have now changed all four notes in this measure to quarter notes (see Figure 4-7).

Figure 4-7

Finale advances the editing frame to the next measure, as in Figure 4-7, when the F eighth note's duration became a quarter note, and is ready to continue with note entry.

You can turn off the auto-advance feature (Jump To Next Measure); its function is to advance to the next measure when the previous one is rhythmically full.

When a triplet or tuplet is at the end of a measure and you do not use the Option-3 method but use the Tuplet Tool itself, you may want to turn Jump To Next Measure off.

• Select Jump To Next Measure from the Speedy menu. Make sure that the Jump To Next Measure command has toggled and no longer has a check mark in the menu. This disables the auto-advance feature. Now that you have turned the Jump To Next Measure feature off, you can use the ( ]) /([ ]) key to move to the next measure.

Whenever you change a note's duration (or enter a new note), the insertion bar moves to the right, ready for you to enter a new note or rest (or to change the rhythmic value of an existing note).

Changing a Note's Pitch

To change a note's pitch, position the cursor precisely on the notehead. Drag the F from the example in Figure 4-7 to the F line an octave higher. In Speedy Entry, you can move notes to other pitches by simply dragging them. (If your MIDI keyboard or synthesizer module is connected properly, Finale will play the note's pitch each time it changes.)

• Click squarely on the high F's notehead. With the button down, drag it slightly to the right or left. The Speedy Entry Tool gives you complete control of both a note's pitch and its measure position.

To drag a note only horizontally (so that you cannot drag it off of its pitch), or vertically (so that you can't drag its position left or right), press the Shift key while dragging the notehead in the desired direction. This is important if you do not want to change the horizontal position of a note, only its pitch.

• Move the insertion bar to the third note in the measure (the E). Remember, you move the insertion bar by pressing the arrow keys or by clicking on a note.

Deleting and Restoring a Note

Press the Delete key/Shift+(.) to remove a note, rest, or entire chord from your score.

What if you delete a note by accident?

Anytime you are working with the Speedy Entry Tool, remember that you can always undo your last action by pressing ⌘-Z/Ctrl+Z (the keyboard equivalent for the Undo command in the Edit menu).

Press ⌘-Z/Ctrl+Z. The note you deleted reappears.

Creating Chords

Entering Chord Notes

- Position the insertion bar on the F that you moved an octave higher in the section "Changing a Note's Pitch," and use the up/down arrows to move the crossbar to the third-space C.

- Press Enter. There are now two notes in the chord (see Figure 4-8).

Figure 4-8

Using the four directional arrows, you can maneuver anywhere in a measure, and using the Enter key, you can add a note to an existing note or chord. (If the insertion bar is on a rest, pressing Enter turns the rest into a note.)

Try moving the crossbar up and down the notes of this chord. If you hold down the ⬆ key, Finale will start adding ledger lines, and the measure you are working on will scroll downward (or upward, if you are pressing the ⬇ key).

- Double-click the second-space A of the same chord. This is another way to add a note to a chord.

Deleting Chord Notes

- Use the key to position the crossbar squarely on the top notehead of the chord. Press Clear. Clear removes a note from a chord. (If there is only one note in the chord, Clear will turn it into a rest. The Delete key removes the entire chord.)

Accidentals

Entering Accidentals

- Position the crossbar on the C of the chord from the example in Figure 4-8. Press the plus (+) key on the numeric pad (or Shift + on a laptop). A ♯ will appear. The (+) key adds a ♯ to a note (or raises a ♭ note to a ♮).

- Position the crossbar on the A and press the minus (-) key. The (-) key adds a ♭ to a note (or subtracts a ♯).

Enharmonic Spellings

If a note in the score has been "spelled incorrectly," it is possible to flip to an enharmonic equivalent by using the 9 key.

- Leave the crossbar on the A♭ and press the 9 key. The note will change to a G♯.

- Move the crossbar down away from the two notes. Press the 9 key several times. If the crossbar is on a chord's stem and not on a notehead, pressing the 9 key will cycle a complete chord through its various enharmonic spellings (see Figure 4-9).

Figure 4-9

Hiding Accidentals and Courtesy Accidentals

- For the moment, cycle through until the lower note is an Ab. In the next step, you will hide the accidental.

- Position the crossbar on the Ab. Press the asterisk (*) key. You can use the asterisk key on the numeric keypad. If you prefer, however, you can press Shift-8 (the main keyboard asterisk) instead.

- Press the asterisk key to hide an accidental or insert a courtesy or "cautionary" accidental. Notes retain their identity when played back internally or via MIDI. A note that looks as if it is an A with a hidden accidental (Ab) will still play back as an Ab. To restore a hidden accidental, merely press the asterisk key again. Any note that has a hidden accidental will have a (*) below the note in the edit frame when you click on it, to remind you that it is hidden.

- To add parentheses around a courtesy accidental, press the (P) key. A second press will remove the parentheses.

Inserting Notes or Rests

- Create a new score with the example in Figure 4-9. Position the insertion bar on the two-note chord and remove it by pressing Delete.

- Move the insertion bar back to the middle C note again. While holding down Shift, press the 6 key. When you press Shift, Finale will insert a note or rest just before the insertion bar—Shift-6 is the keyboard equivalent of the half-note value. (If you had held down a key on your synthesizer while you pressed Shift-6, you would have inserted a note instead of a rest.)

The problem is that there are five beats in the measure—the half rest and three quarter notes. If you have turned off Finale's rhythmic-watchdog feature (Jump To Next Measure), Finale will not notify you until you exit the editing frame.

To change a note to a rest put the cursor on the note and press the Clear key or Shift-Delete.

If you are a laptop user, you should get used to using the Shift key for Speedy Entry commands, as laptops do not usually have the separate calculator section of the keyboard.

- Press the zero key/(0) to exit the editing frame. Finale displays a dialog box that tells you that there are too many beats in the measure.

There are multiple methods of solving this problem:

Leave the extra beats in the measure (by selecting the top option).

Tell Finale to eliminate any extra beats by removing them from the end of the measure (by clicking the second radio button).

Tell Finale to insert any extra notes that it removes from the end of this measure into the beginning of the *following* measure (by clicking the third button).

Tell Finale to rebar the music by redistributing notes throughout the staff until no measure contains more beats than are allowed by the time signature (see "Rebarring Music" in the *Finale Online Support*).

- Click "Delete the extra notes," and then click OK. Finale will eliminate the extra beat—the last E quarter note—and you will exit the editing frame.

- Position the insertion bar on the C and press the period (.) key. Finale will add a dot to the note. You can add up to 10 dots to a note or rest.

- Position the insertion bar on the D, and then press the 4 key. You will turn the last quarter note into an eighth note; the measure is now rhythmically complete.

Layering with Speedy Entry Input

In contrapuntal music two different voices can occupy the same staff with different stem directions and rhythmic values. Notes that are stem up are almost invariably the upper voices, while downstem notes usually operate as the lower voices. Let's start a new example and use the **Layer Function** in Speedy Entry.

Creating Layer 1

- Input the line from Figure 4-10.

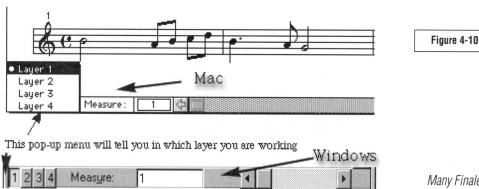

Figure 4-10

Mac

This pop-up menu will tell you in which layer you are working

Windows

If you click and drag in the Layer display field, you can select one of four possible layers to work with in a pull-down submenu.

As a rule, start your higher-pitched line in Layer 1 and the lower-pitched line in Layer 2. When you enter the Layer 2 entry frame after inserting Layer 1, all the previously entered notes in Layer 1 entries will become gray so that you can still see them (see Figure 4-11).

Many Finale users make the mistake of trying to edit a Layer 1 voice while in the Layer 2 edit frame, which is not possible. So if you have a note that cannot be edited, make sure you are working in the proper layer. You can have up to four layers in each staff.

Figure 4-11

Creating Layer 2

Enter the Layer 2 line, and the stems will automatically format to the proper direction, including unison notes (see Figure 4-12).

Figure 4-12

If you have created an additional measure at the end of the example or any score, it is simple to delete a measure or any number of measures by selecting the Mass Mover Tool and selecting the measure(s), then pressing Delete/Backspace (see Figure 4-12).

When you hold down the shift key and the up and down arrow you can easily shift up or down a layer/not available in Windows.

Selecting Display Colors

One of the implementations of Finale is the ability to assign color to various screen elements. This function can make it very easy to identify each layer, especially if you assign them exclusive colors.

- Go to the View Menu and choose the **Select Display Colors** command (Figure 4-13).

View Options Window

✓ Scroll View ⌘`
Page View ⌘`

Home Position ⌘H
Redraw Screen ⌘D
Redraw Options...
Select Display Colors...

Figure 4-13

The Select Display Colors dialog box will appear. Simply click on any of the buttons in this dialog box to bring up the standard Macintosh or Windows color selection dialog box. Note all the score item possibilities for colorization in Figure 4-14.

By differentiating the colors of different layers in a contrapuntal piece of music, it is possible to create or project a visual analysis of a work.

To use color coding of Finale information, you must select the Use Colors box in the lower left-hand part of the display. When you click on one of the item color buttons, a standard color dialog box appears for your choice (see Figure 4-15).

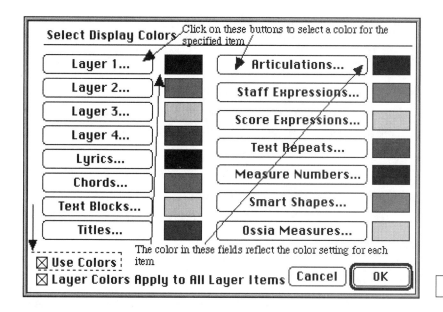

Figure 4-14

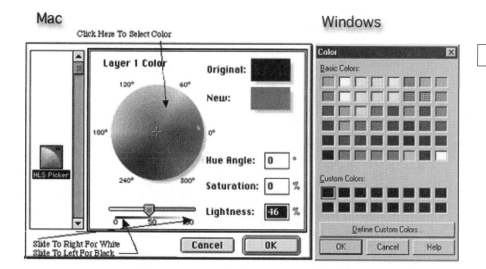

Figure 4-15

The Windows version of the color picker is slightly different in appearance but functions exactly the same. Color scores can be printed with a color printer.

This can be a valuable educational tool, such as illustrating fugue entrances. Some very expensive scores of Bach's work were colorized in this manner when printed.

Colorization also makes determining which layer, articulation, etc. you are editing easier when each one has a different screen color.

Building a Single Staff Score with Speedy Entry

You've now learned the basics of using the Speedy Entry Tool with the MIDI keyboard. You have learned how to enter notes rapidly, change their values, change their pitches, add rests, insert notes, add dots, and move around the score using the right and left bracket keys.

Using your knowledge of the Speedy Entry Tool, enter "Frere Jacques" as indicated in Drill 4-A. For the moment, however, do not enter any music past measure 1. Review the Speedy Entry keyboard commands you have learned so far.

Notice that the song "Frere Jacques" has many measures that are the same or repetitions. Measures 1 and 2 are exactly the same, as are measures 3 and 4. To save time, you can use the Mass Mover Tool's copying function to complete the melody.

4-A Measure Setup/Copying: "Frere Jacques"

1. Create eight measures with the Measure Tool.

2. Input the first measure of notes as in Figure 4-16 and select the Mass Mover Tool.

Figure 4-16

3. Select the first measure by dragging the measure so that its image is superimposed on measure 2 (see Figure 4-17).

Figure 4-17

4. You can then answer the dialog box as to how many copies of the selected measure you wish to copy (Figure 4-18).

Figure 4-18

5. Complete the melody using the copy feature of the Mass Mover Tool. The measures in the boxes will be the sources to drag to the following measures to copy (see Figure 4-19). Always analyze your music to see if there are any repeated melodies to make your input job easier.

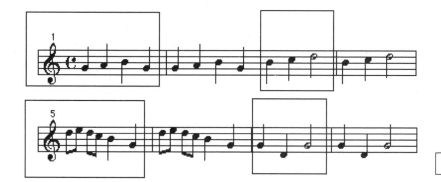

Figure 4-19

Multiple Measure Copy

To finish the song in Drill 4-A, you would need to copy the entire melody twice. However, the dragging trick only works when you can see both source and target measures on the screen at the same time. In this case, then, Finale has a copying shortcut that can be used to copy any amount of music from one place to another, even when the source and the target are hundreds of measures apart.

Your goal is to select measures 1 through 8. Since you can drag-enclose only what fits on a single screen, you cannot select all eight measures by drag-enclosing or creating a marquee unless you have a large monitor. You need another way to select measures.

• Click anywhere on a blank part of the screen to remove the highlighting.

Selecting Several Measures by Shift-Clicking

There is a common computer trick for selecting large amounts of material—
in word processors, spreadsheets, and even music programs. It's called
Shift-clicking, and it works in the following way (see Figure 4-20):

Click Here ⟶ Scroll to the endpoint ⟶ Shift Click here.

Figure 4-20

Everything between these measures is selected

You can use this technique to select the eight measures you are going
to copy.

- Click on measure 1. Click the right scroll bar arrow until measure 8
  comes into view.

While pressing the Shift key, click on measure 8. Measures 1 through 8
are now selected.

Copying Music to Off-Screen Targets

Now you need to copy this music to the end of the piece—but you
obviously cannot do it by dragging the highlighted measures onto the target measures, since the target measures are not even on the screen.

Here's another keyboard shortcut:

- Drag the scroll box until the counter says Measure: 9. You might find it
  quicker to type 9 into the measure counter, and then press Return.

While pressing Option-Shift simultaneously, click on measure 9. That's a
very useful trick to remember: Option-Shift-clicking the target measures is
the same as dragging the image of the source measures onto the target
measures.

A box appears, asking how many times you want the material copied.
Indicate "once."

Click OK or press Return. That's all there is to it! You have copied the
melody for your first lead sheet.

Speedy Entry Shortcuts

Combining the speed of Speedy Entry with the convenience of Mass Mover copying is a quick, accurate method of entering music, particularly with practice.

To enter several repeated notes, hold the synthesizer key down continuously while you repeatedly press the rhythmic-value keys (you do not have to restrike the synthesizer key each time). Music is only entered when you press a rhythmic-value key, so feel free to play your synthesizer as much as you like, without inadvertently throwing notes onto the screen.

Chord entry is simple: Hold down the synthesizer keys for *all* the notes in the chord before you press the rhythmic-value key.

You can drag any note of a chord up or down to change its pitch, just as you did with a single note earlier in this chapter.

You can drag an entire chord up and down the staff (instead of dragging one note at a time) by double-clicking and, on the second click, holding the button down.

You can also drag any note or chord horizontally. If you want to drag a note only vertically or only horizontally, press Shift while you drag—your cursor will be "constrained" to vertical or horizontal movements.

Breaking Beams: If you position the insertion bar on the second of two notes that are beamed together, pressing the slash key (/)/(/) will break the beam; pressing it again will rejoin the beam.

Grace Notes: There is also a key that turns any note into a grace note (and back again, like a toggle)—the semicolon (;)/(;).

Ties: Pressing the equal (=)/(=) key ties a note to the next note. You can tie all notes of a chord at once by positioning the crossbar on the chord stem.

Moving the Edit Frame Vertically: If you are working on a score with several staves, press the Return key/Return key to move the editing frame down to the next lower staff; press Shift-Return to move it back up.

Hiding an Entry: If you ever want to hide an entry (a note or rest), just position the insertion bar on it and press the letter O/O key; the entry will disappear.

Adding Articulations

You use the **Articulation Tool** ⟦⟧ for inputting articulations. When you select this tool, double-click in the score where you want an articulation to appear, and then select the appropriate articulation. Articulations can also be programmed to effect MIDI playback, such as the staccato dot shortening note playback durations. The articulation designer can be used to customize and create articulations. This is beyond the scope of this book, but can be explored in your Finale Manual.

Adding Dynamics

You use the **Staff Expression Tool** ⟦⟧ for inputting dynamics or staff expressions. When you select this tool, double-click and select the appropriate dynamic or marking. There is also a **Score Expression Tool** that will allow you to add dynamics or a staff expression to all staves at once.

Adding Smart Shapes

You use the **Smart Shape Tool** ⟦⟧ for inputting slurs and crescendos/decrescendos. When you select this tool, double-click below or above the music and drag left or right to set the appropriate length.

Erasing Music ⟦⟧

There may be times when you need to erase some of your music. Following is a quick way to do it. If you are not already at the beginning of the song, choose Home Position from the View menu before proceeding.

- Click the Mass Mover Tool ⟦⟧.

- Select the first two measures of the song. You can use any of the selection methods you have tried so far: clicking one measure and then Shift-clicking the second, or drag-enclosing both at once.

- Press Clear/Delete. The measures are now empty, but not deleted from the score.

Suppose you really did not want to erase the first two measures of the song. Fortunately, you can always recover from any Mass Mover Tool action by choosing Undo from the Edit menu. Finale will restore the music to the first two measures.

Barlines

The thin vertical lines drawn through the staff to set off the time-length of each measure are called barlines. *They enclose, so to speak, the requisite number of beats or pulsations, whether in unchanging sequence (unaltered time signature) or in changing sequence (when the meter is variable).*

In their earliest forms, barlines had more the character of breathing points, of places of brief rest for the singers, than of fixed indications of metrical pattern. Regularly recurring barlines in the modern sense first appeared in the keyboard tablature notation of the fifteenth century. This symbol now functions to define the meter in two ways: it marks the primary stresses, as the first beat following any barline receives the strongest pulsation of the measure; and it divides the basic pulse into convenient groups, or units of time.

Imprecise musicians use the terms bar and measure synonymously, but—strictly speaking—they are not the same. A bar is the barline itself, not the measure set off by two barlines.

Grouping Staves with Barlines

1. Keyboard instrument (piano, celesta, harpsichord) and harp—the barline goes through both staves.

2. Organ—the barline goes through the two manual staves and stops: then separately through the pedal staff.

3. Ensembles (string quartet, woodwind trio, brass quintet, etc.)—the barline goes through all staves.

4. Orchestra and band scores—the barlines go through each section (woodwinds, brasses, percussion, and strings), breaking between the separate choirs.

5. Chorus and vocal ensembles—the barlines go through each voice staff only, and are not joined. This is to avoid running the barlines into the text, placed between the staves.

The double bar consists of two vertical lines of equal size, placed very slightly apart on the staff and used principally to indicate the end of a section of music.

The period form of the double bar, used at the end of a composition of a movement within it, consists of a thin vertical line followed by a thicker one. In itself this double bar means the end. It is redundant, then to put Fine over or under the final double bar.

—From *Music Notation*, pp. 182-185

Formatting Measures

Adding Blank Measures at the End of a Document

To add a single measure at the end of the score, Option-click the Measure Tool.

Inserting Blank Measures within a Score

* Click the Measure Tool 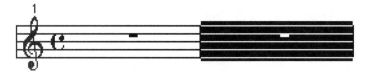 .

* Click the measure following the point where a measure(s) is to be inserted (see Figure 4-21). Select the Measure pull-down command from the Main Menu.

Figure 4-21

Even if there is more than one staff in your score, simply click a single measure. Finale will add a blank measure in every staff.

* From the Measures submenu of the Measure menu, choose **Insert**. A box will appear, asking how many measures you want to insert (see Figure 4-22).

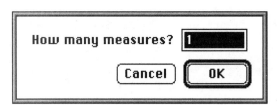

Figure 4-22

- Enter the desired number of measures. Click OK (or press Return).

Removing Measures

- Click the Mass Mover Tool and select a region.

- If you want to remove the measures from the score, press Delete. (You can also choose Delete from the Measures submenu of the Mass Edit menu.) This will remove the selected measures from every staff, even if only one is selected. Therefore, your score will contain fewer measures.

Measure Numbers

You can create different regions of measure numbers in your score, each with:

Different fonts

Different positions

Different numbering schemes and with or without enclosures

An appearance at only specific places in the score (serving as rehearsal numbers)

To create or edit measure numbers, double-click the **Measure Tool** ▤. The Measure Number dialog box will appear (Figure 4-23[B]).

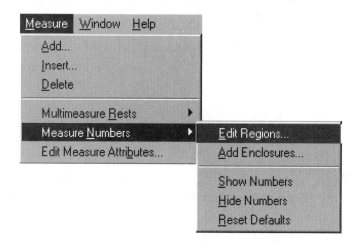

Figure 4-23(A)

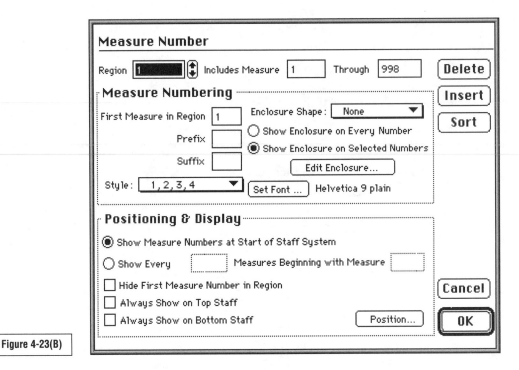

Figure 4-23(B)

- Enter the Start Measure and End Measure for this selected region (see Figure 4-24).

Figure 4-24

The start and end measures are the actual measures in the piece; they have nothing to do with what numbering arrangement you define. A score may have several different measure number regions.

If you want to define a region to number only part of the piece, the Through field is the measure *immediately following* the last measure to be numbered. For example, if the piece begins with an anacrusis measure, you will probably want what is actually measure 2 to be numbered as measure 1; if so, type 2 into the First Measure in Region box (see Figure 4-25).

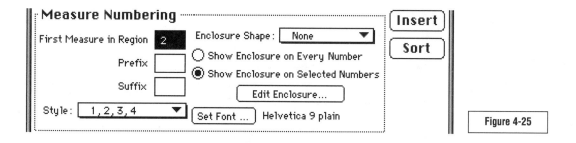

Figure 4-25

The First Measure in Region will display the number selected for the beginning of a region. If you had typed in 5, then the region's first measure would start with five and number the remaining measures sequentially.

A Prefix number or letter entered in the Prefix box will create a measure number region with a sequence of prefix labeled and numbered measures. For example, if you entered A into the Prefix field, measure numbers would appear as A1, A2, A3, etc. in the score. By typing in a letter or other character in the Prefix or Suffix fields, you get the following results (see Figure 4-26):

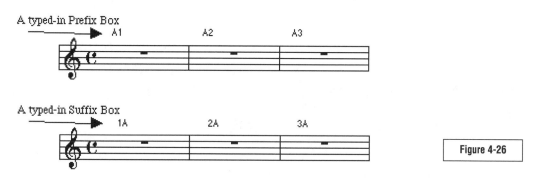

Figure 4-26

- Click Set Font to choose a font and style for this selected region (see Figure 4-27 [A]).

Figure 4-27(A)

The Style pop-up menu has the following numbering options (Figure 4-27 [B]):

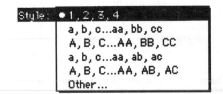

Figure 4-27(B)

Font parameters are defined in the usual way.

When Show Measure Numbers at Start of Staff System is selected, a measure number will only appear at the beginning of a new system (see Figure 4-28).

Positioning & Display

◉ Show Measure Numbers at Start of Staff System

○ Show Every [   ] Measures Beginning with Measure [   ]

Figure 4-28

To specify the frequency of the numbers, click the Show Every radio button and in the field next to it select the number of measure desired. 1 = every measure, 2 = every two measures, 5 = every five measures, etc. The Measures Beginning with Measure field defines the start number of the region.

The options in Figure 4-29 define measure number placement above the staff or below the staff.

☐ Hide First Measure Number in Region
☐ Always Show on Top Staff
☐ Always Show on Bottom Staff

[Position...]   [Cancel]   [OK]

Figure 4-29

If you click the Show Enclosure on Selected Numbers radio button, no measure numbers will be enclosed (see Figure 4-30). When you return to the score, simply double-click the number's handle to add the enclosure you specified to a particular measure number. Then you will use the Enclosure Designer to select the parameters for your enclosure (see Figure 4-31).

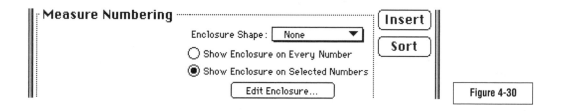

Figure 4-30

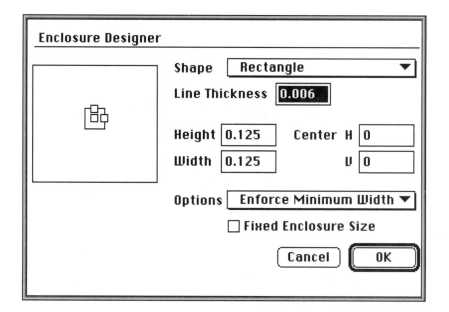

Figure 4-31

Figure 4-32 illustrates the possible enclosure shapes you can select from the Enclosure Shape pull-down menu.

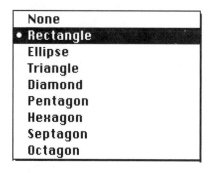

Figure 4-32

Figure 4-33 shows the measure number with its selected shape.

Figure 4-33

You can have multiple shapes in a region (see Figure 4-34).

Figure 4-34

When you do not want the measure numbers to begin with 1, enter a number in the First Measure in Region text box (Figure 4-35). The number in this text box tells Finale how many measures come before the Start Measure.

Figure 4-35

- Click the Position button, shown in Figure 4-36.

Figure 4-36

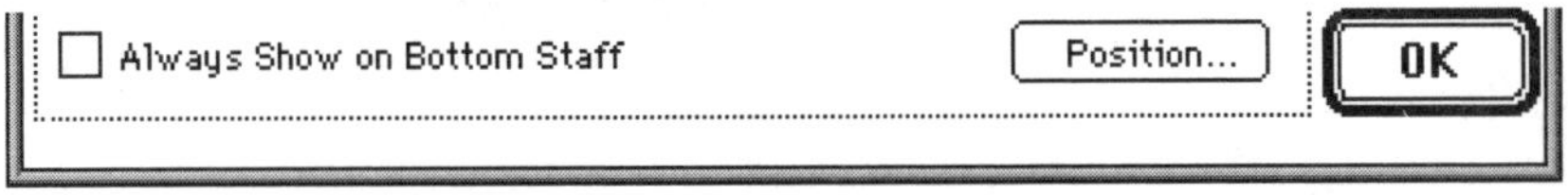

- Drag the measure number in the dialog box to the position desired (Figure 4-37). All the measure numbers will now be placed in that position, until a new region is defined.

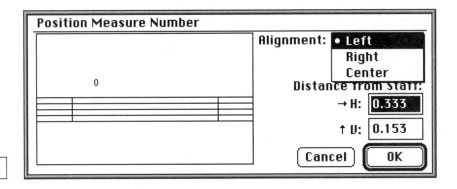

Figure 4-37

To set up the parameters for another region, click the up arrow (Figure 4-38).

To create a region before the current one, click Insert. To remove a region, click Delete (Figure 4-39).

Figure 4-38

Figure 4-39

Removing Measure Numbers from a Staff

- Click the Staff Tool ⊞, and double-click the staff whose numbers you want to remove. The Staff Attributes dialog box will appear.

- In the "Items to Display" section, click Measure Numbers to deselect it. Click OK (or press Return). This option is helpful in a large score where you only want measure numbers on the top staff of the entire system or the bottom staff.

Moving a Measure Number

- If the measure number handles are not present, click the Measure Tool ⊟. A handle will appear on each measure number in the score.

- Drag a number by its handle to reposition it. Select it and press the arrow keys to "nudge" it for fine adjustment.

Professional looking scores only have measure numbers on the top or bottom stances. Use this technique to eliminate measure numbers in the middle.

Measure Repeat Signs

Repetition is one of the most venerable devices for unifying a musical composition. Its ancient status has so well consolidated notational practice that the few symbols are easy to learn and unmistakable in their meaning.

Repetitions may affect single units of time (beats), whole measures of any length, and groups of measures. Each length of repetition has its own distinctive symbol and employs this symbol exclusively.

—From *Music Notation*, p. 223

The measure repeat symbol [✕], often used in rhythm parts, dictates that the measure in which it appears is to be a repetition of the previous measure (see Figure 4-40).

Figure 4-40

- To create a measure repeat sign, input the first measure of Figure 4-40. Click the Staff Tool and select measure 2.

- From the Staff menu, choose Apply Staff Styles. The Alternate Notation dialog box will appear (see Figure 4-41).

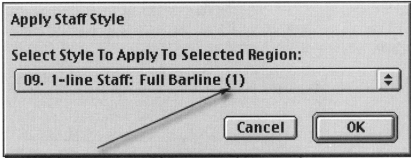

Figure 4-41

Number or Letter Of Programed Metatool

- Scroll to select "One-Bar Repeat(s)" or "Two-Bar Repeat(s)." Click OK. Finale will hide all the music, and replace it with the selected measure repeat marks, in this case the two-bar repeat (Figure 4-42).

Figure 4-42

To restore the music, choose the measures again, choose Alternate Notation from the Staff menu, and select Normal Notation (M).

- By using the Shift Key and any number or letter key, you can program
  your own Metatool Macro.

The Repeat Tool

In Finale, a repeat barline is simply a sign that directs the continuity of the
music, including:

Playback to another measure

The coda sign, which makes the music jump to a later measure

Nested repeats

Infinite loops

Purely graphic repeat barlines without playback functions

4-B Using the Repeat Tool

In this drill we will create a first and second ending.

1. Create Figure 4-43 as a Finale document.

Figure 4-43

2. When you have finished inputting the above diagram, use the Staff Tool
   and drag the staff handle to a lower position on your screen. This will
   give you enough room to view and position the first and second
   endings.

3. Click on the **Repeat Tool** , then click on measure 2. The Repeat
   Selection dialog box will appear, displaying four icons at the top (Figure
   4-44):

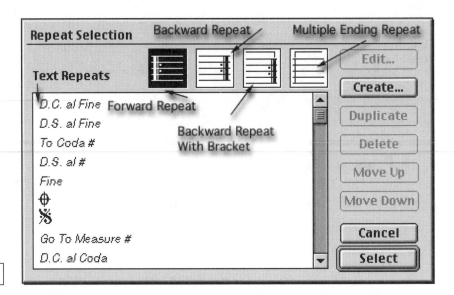

Figure 4-44

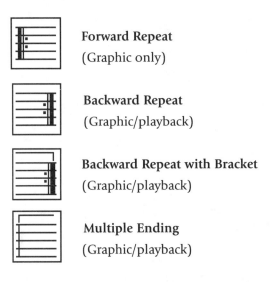

Forward Repeat
(Graphic only)

Backward Repeat
(Graphic/playback)

Backward Repeat with Bracket
(Graphic/playback)

Multiple Ending
(Graphic/playback)

4. The barline on the left, the Forward Repeat, is the one you want (see Figure 4-44). Click on it. When you return to the score, the barline will be in place.

A Forward Repeat is purely graphic. Finale stores all playback information for a particular repetition in the backward repeat barline (at the end of a repeated section).

5. Click on measure 3. The next repeat barline will direct the playback to return to measure 2. This barline will be part of the first ending, so you will need the Backward Repeat with Bracket (see Figure 4-45).

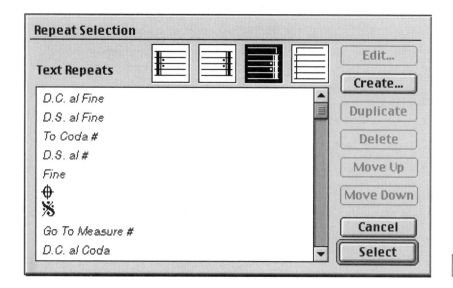

Figure 4-45

6. Double-click the Backward Repeat with Bracket (the third icon) or click the Select button, which does the same function.

7. The Backward Repeat Bar Assignment box will appear, requesting details about the playback definition of the repeat barline (see Figure 4-46).

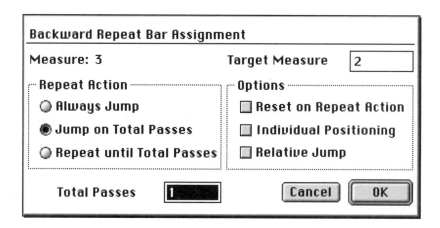

Figure 4-46

8. To create a graphic barline with no playback function, click OK (or press Return) at this point. Since we want playback, for the field Total Passes, type 1. You typed a 1 because the music in this measure (3) is only played once; thereafter, the playback jumps to the second ending.

A simple rule for using the Backward Repeat with Bracket barline: The number in the Total Passes box should match the numbers you would put in the Ending text box (see Step 12).

9. Also click "Jump on Total Passes." In the next step you will create a special barline at the beginning of the first ending that will be responsible for directing the music to the second ending, skipping over this ending completely.

Select the Target Measure Field to 2. This specifies the target measure the repeat sign will return to. This is the measure you placed the graphic forward repeat in.

10. Click OK (or press Return). The repeat will be placed into your score.

Note: If you were creating a first ending that was several measures long, you would want to stretch this bracket to the left. Finale will not let you drag it more than a half inch or so, however, unless you double-click its handle and select Individual Positioning in the dialog box. (Individual Positioning also lets you drag the bracket that appears in each staff individually.) It is not necessary to stretch it now, but keep the Individual Positioning feature in mind.

If you intend to make use of the Repeat Tool's playback capabilities, study the following terminology:

Target Measure: The Target Measure is the measure to which Finale jumps, or directs playback, when it performs the repeat. In the case of this example, the Target Measure is 2. If a Target Measure value of zero is input, then the barline will not affect playback.

Total Passes: The number you type into this box tells Finale how high it should count or how many times it should play the music up to this point before performing one of the following three Repeat Actions:

Always Jump: This option ignores any number in the Total Passes box. In this case Finale will jump to the target measure *every* time it reaches this repeat barline.

Jump on Total Passes: Finale will only jump to the target measure when the playback reaches this barline the number of times specified in the Total Passes box.

Repeat Until Total Passes: This is a "first ending" option, because it tells Finale not to play past this measure until it's been played for the *second* time, or whatever number that is specified in the Total Passes box.

11. Double-click measure 3. This time, select the front bracket (Multiple Ending Repeat) for the first ending (Figure 4-47).

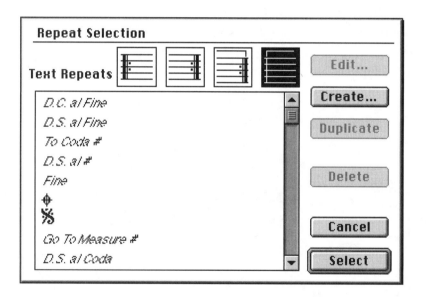

Repeat Selection

Text Repeats

D.C. al Fine
D.S. al Fine
To Coda #
D.S. al #
Fine
⊕
𝄋
Go To Measure #
D.S. al Coda

Edit...
Create...
Duplicate
Delete
Cancel
Select

Figure 4-47

12. When the Ending Repeat Bar Assignment dialog box appears (Figure 4-48), type in a 1 and period, set the "Target Measure" field to 4, then click on OK.

Ending Repeat Bar Assignment

Ending Text (Optional)

> 1.

Target Measure `4`   **Total Passes** `1`

☐ **Individual Positioning**   ☐ **Multiple...**
☐ **Jump if Ignoring Repeats**
☐ **Relative Jump**   [Cancel] [OK]

Figure 4-48

13. Double-click on measure 4. Now we are going to create the second ending.

14. Double-click the Multiple Ending Repeat (the rightmost icon) (Figure 4-49). The Ending Repeat Bar Assignment box comes up; all you need to do now is to create a purely graphic bracket for the second ending. In the Ending Text box, type 2 and a period. You can leave all the other elements of this dialog box alone, since this bracket does not have playback capabilities (see Figure 4-50).

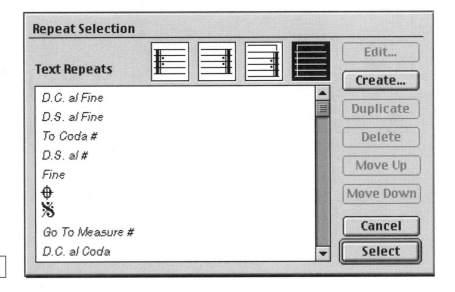

Repeat Selection

Text Repeats

[Edit...]
[Create...]

D.C. al Fine
D.S. al Fine
To Coda #
D.S. al #
Fine
⊕
𝄋
Go To Measure #
D.C. al Coda

[Duplicate]
[Delete]
[Move Up]
[Move Down]
[Cancel]
[Select]

Figure 4-49

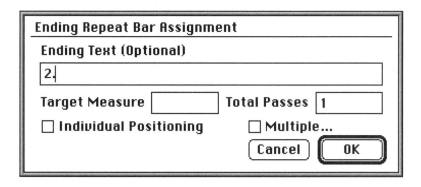

Ending Repeat Bar Assignment

Ending Text (Optional)

2.

Target Measure [   ]   Total Passes [1   ]

☐ Individual Positioning   ☐ Multiple...

[Cancel]   [OK]

Figure 4-50

15. Click OK (or press Return). Now both "repeats" are in your score (see Figure 4-51). To adjust repeat bracket heights, click the measure again (handles appear), and then drag the bracket handles up or down. That's all there is to creating a practical set of first and second endings.

Figure 4-51

Check your example aurally. Use the Playback controls.

To remove a repeat barline or bracket, click the Repeat Tool, then click the measure. Click the square handle at the bottom of the barline and press Delete.

Chapter Four Review

Using the tools in Chapter Four, you now know how to input notes with Speedy Entry and manipulate your Finale score in the following ways:

By using Speedy Entry with MIDI and all keyboard shortcuts

By creating layers

By using the Mass Mover Tool for copying measures

By modifying measure numbers

By creating graphic and text repeats

Notes

Chapter Four Projects

1. Create a separate document for each section of this project, Project 4-1A and 4-1B.

1A.

Hint:

Time Signature

1B.

2. Open a new document and save as "Project 4-2." Create the following score with multiple layers.

3. "Frere Jacques" Open a new document and save as "Project 4-3."
Create the following score using the Mass Mover Tool and add
articulations and dynamics.

4. Open a new document and save as "Project 4-4." Create the
following score using the Repeat Tool.

5. Open a new document and save as "Project 4-5." Create the
following score with layers and special measure numbers.

Hint: Pay attention to the clef sign.

CHAPTER FIVE

Creating
a Lead Sheet

A *lead sheet* is a basic form of sheet music containing three elements:

1. Melody

2. Lyrics

3. Accompanying chord symbols

Often, lead sheets are named fake sheets because their accompaniment is faked or improvised, with the chords and song form used as a structure for improvised solos. The term *fakebook* relates to a collection of standards and jazz original fake sheets.

With the above definition in mind, you will create a lead sheet for the song "Bill Bailey." This will help you learn insertion of lyrics, chord symbols, and guitar diagrams to create a simple musical score in lead sheet form.

5-A Creating a Lead Sheet

1. Open the file "Bill Bailey Excerpt" that you created in Chapter Three, Drill 3-A.

2. Or, create the musical example of "Bill Bailey" in Figure 5-1 from scratch.

3. Save this score as "Bill Bailey Excerpt."

4. Analyze the example, noting measures where the melody repeats. Use the Mass Mover Tool to copy these measures.

Figure 5-1

Entering Lyrics into a Score

One of Finale's greatest strengths is its skillful ability to handle lyrics. If you provide lyrics with hyphenation between syllables, Finale can automatically distribute them to the melody line. Finale will center every syllable under its melody note. If notes are moved horizontally, then the syllable will move with it, and automatically avoid ties and rests.

There are two ways to create lyrics within Finale:

You can type the lyrics directly into the score, called **Type Into Score**

You can use the faster **Click Assignment** method—where you type the lyrics in Finale's text processor and insert them into the score all at once

The Click Assignment method also offers the option of pasting lyrics into Finale's text processor from another program, such as a word processing program.

In this chapter, you will try both techniques.

"Type into Score" Lyric Entry

- Click on the **Lyrics Tool** 🐟 . A new menu, called **Lyrics**, will appear.

- Choose **Type Into Score** from the Lyrics menu (see Figure 5-2 [A]). A row of four positioning triangles will appear at the left edge of the screen (see Figure 5-2 [B]).

- Click anywhere *within* the staff lines above the first note. A small blinking cursor or insertion point will appear immediately under the first note.

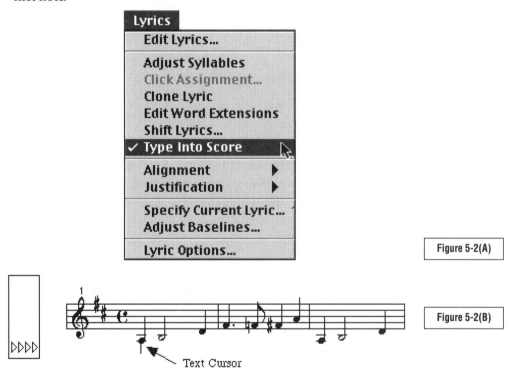

Figure 5-2(A)

Figure 5-2(B)

Text Cursor

Each time you type a *space* or a *hyphen*, Finale will automatically move the insertion point to the next note in preparation for entering the next syllable. Finale will automatically scroll the music as you enter the lyrics. This will help maintain your place in the score. When working with lyrics, there are some special features available:

Press the Delete key to remove a mistake in the lyrics

A backspace to the previous syllable (Delete key)/Backspace will highlight the entire syllable, allowing you to replace it all at once with the first new text letter

Clicking in the staff above a questionable syllable will highlight it for correction. The space bar will skip over sustained notes and rests

- Type: *Won't you come home, Bill Bai-ley, won't you come home? She moans the whole day long;* into the score. As you type these lyrics, you will notice syllables that are supposed to be held through two melody notes, such as *long* (see Figure 5-3).

Figure 5-3

In such cases, just skip past the sustained note by pressing the space bar. Also use the space bar to skip past rests.

- Finish typing in the verse:

I'll do the cook-ing, dar-ling, I'll pay the rent, I know I've done you wrong.

The four small triangles at the left edge of the screen control the *baseline* of the lyrics—an imaginary line upon which the bottom edges of the lyrics align. If you drag the leftmost triangle, you can move the baseline and attached lyrics up and down.

As you type, Finale stores each syllable in a built-in text processor, the **Edit Lyrics** window.

Editing Lyrics

- Choose **Edit Lyrics** from the Lyrics menu (see Figures 5-4 [A] and [B]). One of Finale's important text features is the fact that the score's lyrics and the Edit Lyrics dialog boxes are dynamically linked. This means that

Be very careful with the four triangles at the left of the screen; each has a different function of lyric alignment. Inappropriate moving of triangles takes time to restore lyric positions.

a change of a lyric in either the score or in the Edit Lyric dialog box will result in a lyric change in the document.

Figure 5-4(A)

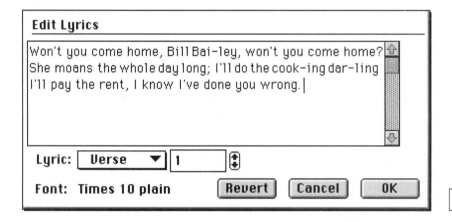

Figure 5-4(B)

- You will need this particular set of lyrics again in a moment, however, so take this opportunity to copy them to the invisible Clipboard.

- Drag through the lyrics so that they are highlighted (click before the first word; without releasing the mouse button, drag to the bottom of the window. You have just selected all the lyrics).

- Press ⌘-C/Ctrl+C. This combination is the keyboard equivalent for the Copy command. Although you do not see that anything has changed, you have placed a copy of these lyrics onto the Clipboard, for later use with Click Assignment of lyrics.

- Click OK to return to the score.

- Choose Home Position from the View menu (or press ⌘-**H**)/Home key. This command returns you to measure 1 of the lead sheet.

While the Type Into Score process is handy, it's not the fastest possible method for entering lyrics. When you are working with very large scores, or when you want to import lyrics from another program (such as a word processor), you might want to use the Click Assignment method. This will allow you to enter the lyrics directly into the Edit Lyrics text processor. No matter which method you prefer, Type Into Score is always handy for making quick changes to lyrics already in the score.

In the next section, you will learn about the Click Assignment method. To restore your melody to its original, wordless form, you'll use Finale's Revert command, which restores your document to the way it was the last time you saved your work.

- Choose **Revert** from the File menu. Finale asks if you are sure you want to revert to the last saved version of the file—the melody before the addition of lyrics, in this case.

- Click OK. Finale now displays your "Bill Bailey" without lyrics.

"Click Assignment" Lyric Entry

With this method, you will enter the complete set of lyrics beforehand in Finale's text processor.

- Choose Edit Lyrics from the Lyrics menu. The Edit Lyrics window is Finale's text processor. Because your document has reverted to the last-saved version, the window is empty. However, remember that you have a full set of lyrics on the Clipboard. All you have to do is paste them into this window.

Press ⌘-**V**/Ctrl+V. This combination is the keyboard equivalent for the Paste command. The lyrics appear in the window, just as though you had typed them. The copy and paste technique you just learned is useful in other contexts, too—for example, you can paste text that you have copied from a word processor. You can also copy and paste lyrics from one place to another within sets of lyrics in Finale.

Editing Lyrics Shortcuts

You can edit your lyrics in the Edit Lyrics window just as you would edit text in any word processor. For example, you can correct mistakes by back-spacing over them with the Delete key. You can copy and paste text as you have just done, using ⌘-**C**/Ctrl+C to copy selected text and ⌘-**V**/Ctrl+V to paste it. You can also cut selected text, so that it's removed from the Edit Lyrics window but placed on the Clipboard, ready for pasting in another place. The Cut command is ⌘-**X**/Ctrl+X.

- Click OK (or press Return). You will return to the score.

Assigning Lyrics

Figure 5-5(A)

Choose **Click Assignment** from the Lyrics menu (Figure 5-5 [A]).

A small, horizontally scrolling window will appear, Figure 5-5 (B), containing the lyrics you just typed. If the window obscures your view of the music, you can use its drag bar to move it to a new location.

The four triangles are again at the left edge of the screen. Remember that these control the baseline of the lyrics. Drag the leftmost triangle up and down to move the lyric line closer to or further from the staff.

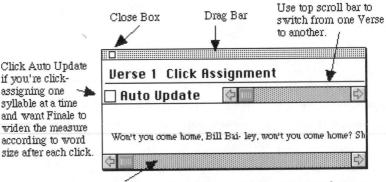

Close Box   Drag Bar   Use top scroll bar to switch from one Verse to another.

Click Auto Update if you're click-assigning one syllable at a time and want Finale to widen the measure according to word size after each click.

Uerse 1 Click Assignment

☐ **Auto Update**

Won't you come home, Bill Bai- ley, won't you come home? Sh

This scroll bar allows you to quickly move to another spot in the lyrics.

Figure 5-5(B)

- Click the cursor *in* the staff on the first melody note.

  The first syllable, "Won't" jumps out of the Click Assignment window and attaches itself to the first note.

- Move the cursor to the second note, and click in the staff. The next syllable is now attached to its note.

  This click-by-click assignment of lyrics can take time when you have lots of lyrics to assign. If you use the Option key, you can distribute all the lyrics with a single click.

- While pressing the Option key, click the third note. Finale will distribute the remaining lyrics into the song automatically.

- Click the Close box in the upper-left corner of the Click Assignment window. Take a moment to scroll through the lead sheet and check Finale's work.

5-B Adding a Second Lyric Line

As it happens, "Bill Bailey" has two verses. This drill will show you how to add multiple verses. Open the file "Bill Bailey."

1. Choose Edit Lyrics from the Lyrics menu. "Lyric: Verse 1" appears in the text window.

2. Click the small arrow beside the Verse pop-up menu to select verse 2 (see Figure 5-6[A]).

Figure 5-6(A)

3. The text window now indicates that Finale is ready for typing in verse 2. To do this, you will create an invisible syllable within the lyrics. When you press the space bar while pressing the Option key, you produce an invisible character called an *Option-space*. Finale thinks of an Option-space as a syllable all by itself, even though it's invisible on the screen. But remember, Finale looks for a *space* or a *hyphen* to indicate that a syllable, invisible or not, has ended; to convince Finale that an option-space is an invisible word, you follow each option-space with a regular space.

4. Type the second verse exactly as you see it below. Create an Option-space where indicated below. Do not forget to type a regular space *before and after* each syllable.

   'Mem-ber that rain-y eve that I drove you out, I am the one to blame; [option-space] [option-space] I'll do the laun-dry ho-ney, I'll take the blame, if you will just come home.

5. Choose Click Assignment from the Lyrics menu. Option-click in the staff above the first note. If you have typed the lyrics correctly, Finale should enter the second verse without a hitch. The option-spaces you added should make all syllables align with their notes.

6. If you need to adjust the positioning of the second lyric line, drag the leftmost of the four positioning handles up or down.

7. Click the Close box of the Click Assignment window.

Type Into Score is also valuable as an analysis or music theory tool. You can type in Roman numerals used in music theory (I, IV, V, Imaj7, iim7, V7, etc.) to create teaching or classroom examples (see Figure 5-6 [B]). Drag the furthest to the left triangle above the staff to place your analysis above the chords.

Figure 5-6(B)

Adding Word Extensions

When a single syllable is sustained for more than one note, it is conventional to add a *word extension*, or extender line, to indicate that it is held beyond the first note. A word extension should only extend to the end of the following note's head, not for the entire note duration value (see Figure 5-7).

Figure 5-7

- Click on the **Lyrics Tool** 🎵, and choose **Edit Word Extensions** from the Lyrics menu. Now you must tell Finale which syllable you want to extend.

- Click in the staff above the syllable "long" (first verse, measure 7). A square handle appears at the end of the corresponding syllable in each verse.

- Drag the top handle to the right until it extends to the next syllable, as shown above. The farther you drag, the longer the underline will be. To remove the underline, click its handle and press Delete.

- Drag the lower handle of the syllable "blame" to the right, too. Repeat the process with the word "wrong" in measure 15 (remember to first click in the staff above the syllable). You will need another word extension on the second-verse syllable "home" (measure 15).

While it's easy enough to add word extensions at any time, remember that word extensions do not grow longer or shorter if the music expands or contracts. Therefore, if you have long word extensions to add, it's a good idea to create them *in Page View*, and only after you have adjusted the page layout of your piece to your satisfaction. For a more complete discussion, see the on-line entry "Lyrics—To Draw a 'Word Extension' Underline."

Chord Symbols and the Chord Tool

Chord symbols (such as D7 or C6) are usually placed over the staff when creating a lead sheet. Frequently only a chord symbol is used in the notation; the actual spacing (or "voicing") of the chord is left up to the player.

Terms Used in Chord Symbol Entry

Library: These are sets of musical symbols, expression markings, and other important musical elements that can be loaded into a document; the user can create or edit new symbols. Libraries can be opened or your personal library saved within the File option in the main Finale menu. There are several chord libraries that are already available.

Chord suffix: The various numerals that follow the pitch letter and indicate extensions of the chord (sevenths and ninths), added notes, or pitch alterations. Editing the chord suffix with Finale is quite easy.

Chord Symbol Entry Methods

In Finale, there are four different methods for adding chord symbols to a score (see Figure 5-8[A]); all four depend on Finale's intelligently reading stacked notes as a specific chord. You select the note or rest in the score that the chord symbol will be above by simply clicking on that note or rest.

Chord
- Manual Input
- ✓Type Into Score
- MIDI Input
- One-Staff Analysis
- Two-Staff Analysis

Figure 5-8(A)

Manual Input - Chord symbols are entered by typing them into a score. If you type in a chord that Finale does not know, it will learn it, and the new suffix will be available if you need the chord again.

Type Into Score - This functions the same as typing lyrics into the score. Click and type into your score. The space bar will move you to the next note for chord entry. The Delete key removes the letter or number of the chord preceding it.

MIDI Input - Chord symbols are automatically entered into the score by playing them individually on a MIDI keyboard. If Finale does not recognize the chord you just played, you can create the proper chord suffix.

One-Staff or Two-Staff Analysis - This will analyze notated chords in a measure of a single staff or two staffs (piano music), respectively, and place an appropriate chord symbol above the staff. If Finale does not recognize the chord it just analyzed, you can create the proper chord identification.

If you do not agree with Finale's labeling of a chord (for example, if it calls a chord "Em7" but you prefer "E7"), you can edit the chord suffix.

Preparing to Enter Chord Symbols

If you are going to add chord symbols to your score, you should prepare your Finale document in three ways:

1. Provide room for chord input, especially if you intend to add guitar chord grids, by using the Staff Tool [icon] to lower the uppermost staff in your page. After you have selected the Staff Tool, hit ⌘-**A**/Ctrl+**A** to select all staves, then move any selected handle to create room for chords at the top of your score.

2. Select the **Open Library** command from the File menu. Load a Chord Suffix Library (unless you are working from the Finale Default File) (see Figure 5-8[B]).

3. Choose a font for the chord letter names. (The font for the suffixes is determined by the Chord Suffix Library you use. In your Libraries folder, there are four such libraries: one each in the New York, Times, Geneva, and Helvetica fonts. You can change chord suffix fonts either globally, by region, or one by one (see Appendix 4).

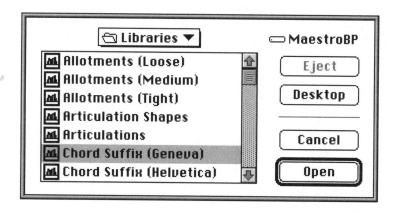

Figure 5-8(B)

Finale offers two systems of chord identification:

Finale will recognize the type of chord it encounters according to the standard rules of chord theory—major, minor, augmented, diminished, suspended, sevenths, ninths, elevenths, and so on (also with alternate bass notes), and place it above the staff

You can easily teach Finale chords that it does not recognize, such as C V/11, or tell Finale to think of a certain chord in a different way. For example, where Finale displays Am7/C, you may prefer C6. Once you have defined a learned chord, Finale will correctly identify it in the future, regardless of the voicing or register, and automatically display the correct symbol

5-C Automatic Chord Symbol Entry: MIDI Input

1. Click on the **Chord Tool** CM7 . The Chord menu will appear at the right of the main menu.

2. Choose MIDI Input from the Chord menu, and then click a note or rest in the score. The ear-shaped cursor appears , indicating that Finale is listening to your MIDI instrument.

3. Create the three-bar phrase in Figure 5-9 (A) in a new document. Click on the C in the second measure (see Figure 5-9 [B]).

Figure 5-9(A)

Figure 5-9(B)

4. Play a C major triad chord, in any register, on your synthesizer; Finale places the chord symbol into the score, aligned with the baseline (controlled by the four triangles at the left side of the screen) (see Figure 5-9 [C]).

Figure 5-9(C)

5. If you do not play the chord in root position, Finale writes it as a chord/bass note; if you play a first inversion C triad (E in the bass) the "C/E" symbol appears in your score (Figure 5-10).

Figure 5-10

If by chance you play two successive chords without moving the cursor, Finale will stack the chord symbols on top of each other. If this occurs, simply click in the chord handle of the undesired chord and press the Delete key.

MIDI Shortcuts

- Play any single key above middle C to advance the ear cursor to the next note position.

- Play any single key below middle C to move the ear cursor backward to the previous note position.

5-D Type Into Score Chord Symbol Entry

Type Into Score chord symbol entry is quite easy to accomplish by simply clicking on a note or rest and typing the root and suffix directly above the staff. Type Into Score is the easiest way to input chords.

1. Click on the **Chord Tool** CM7. From the Chord menu, choose Type Into Score.

2. Create a new Finale document with the following musical example in Figure 5-11.

3. Click on the notes that will contain chords in measures 2 and 3 and type in the root and suffix.

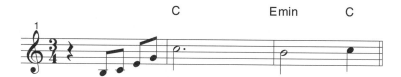

Figure 5-11

5-E Manual Input Chord Symbol Entry

Manual Chord Symbol Entry is also quite easy to accomplish by simply clicking on a note or rest and typing the root and suffix directly into the Chord Symbol field.

1. Click on the Chord Tool CM7. From the Chord menu, choose **Manual Input.**

2. Create a new Finale document with the musical example in Figure 5-12.

3. Place three quarter notes in the first measure and use the Mass Mover Tool to copy the measure to all other measures.

4. Create alternate notation using the Mass Mover Tool.

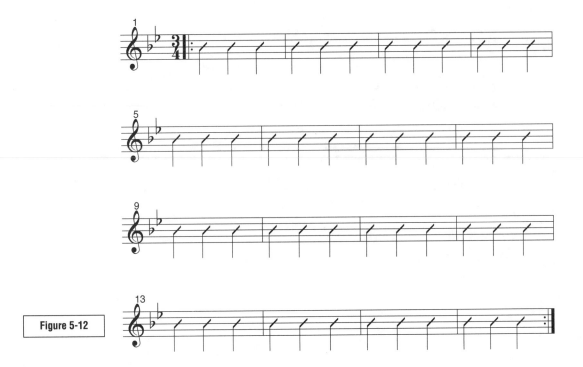

Figure 5-12

5. Click the first slash that the chord symbol is to be centered on. The Chord Definition dialog box will appear (Figure 5-13).

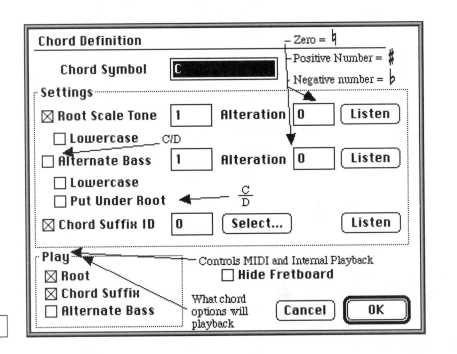

Figure 5-13

6. Enter the root in the Chord Symbol field (Figure 5-14). If you need to alter the scale degree chromatically, type a number into the Alteration boxes. Either a zero, positive, or negative number can be placed into the Alteration box, and will alter the scale tone by half steps.

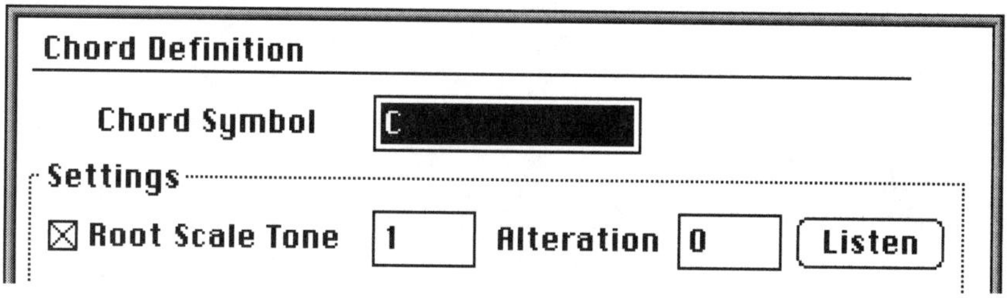

Chord Definition

Chord Symbol `C`

┌ **Settings** ┄┄┄┄┄┄┄┄┄┄┄┄┄┄┄┄┄┄┄┄┄┄┄┄┄┄┄┄┄┄┄┄┄┄┄┄┄┄

☒ **Root Scale Tone** `1`   **Alteration** `0`   [**Listen**]

Figure 5-14

The number after the Root Scale Tone represents the scale degree of your score. 1 = Root, 2 = Sub Mediant, 3 = Mediant, etc. This will allow Finale to understand the relationship of this chord to your score and let you transpose chord symbols with your music.

The scale root numbers will be the same in all keys, but their relationship to the new key will create appropriate new letters and suffix names.

7. The Listen button [**Listen**] will allow you to play the root of the chord into the dialog box. Simply click on it and play the root on your MIDI controller.

8. If there is a different bass note, click on the Alternate Bass box and enter its scale tone in the text box. For an E♭ min6/B chord in the key of B♭ for example, the Root Scale Tone (E♭) is 4, the Alternate Bass is 1, and a positive 1 in the Alteration field creates the B♮ (see Figure 5-15).

☒ **Alternate Bass** `4`   **Alteration** `1`   [**Listen**]

Figure 5-15

Some arrangers prefer to create polychords, with the root directly under the triad. When the Put Under Root box is checked, the chord will be created with the following result (see Figures 5-16 and 5-17):

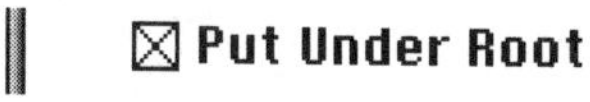

☒ **Put Under Root**

Figure 5-16

Creating a Lead Sheet

Without the Put Root Under Chord Checked

C/D

With the Put Under Root Box Checked

$\dfrac{C}{D}$

Figure 5-17

9. Click on the Chord Suffix ID and then the Select button (Figure 5-18).

Figure 5-18

☒ **Chord Suffix ID** | 0 | (Select...)   (Listen)

10. The Chord Suffix Selection box appears (Figure 5-19). Click on the desired suffix. If there are no suffixes in the palette, either click Create to create a new suffix, or load a chord-suffix library from the File menu. Click Select or press the Return key.

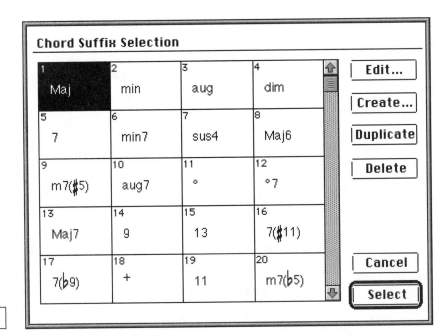

Figure 5-19

11. If you do not desire the chord symbol to play with MIDI or internal playback, click to deselect the Root, Chord Suffix, or Alternate Bass boxes to control the manner of the chord symbol's playback.

12. Click OK (or press the Return key).

5-F Creating a Rhythm / Instrument Chart

1. Add the indicated chords to the musical example in Figure 5-20.

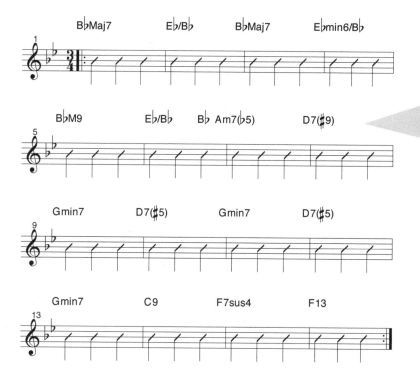

Chords will only attach to notes or rests in a measure. If the default rest is in a measure without either a note or rest, you cannot attach a chord. This also applies to measures before you use alternate notation. If there are notes or rests in the measure before alternate notation, you can attach chords to them.

Figure 5-20

One-Staff Analysis

If you want Finale to analyze a chord notated in the score, choose One-Staff Analysis from the Chord menu, and then click on the chord (see Figure 5-21[A]).

Finale immediately analyzes the chord you have clicked, and places the

```
Chord
  Manual Input
  Type Into Score
  MIDI Input
✓ One-Staff Analysis
  Two-Staff Analysis
  Chord Style            ▶
  Left-Align Chords
  Show Guitar Fretboards
✓ Position Chords
  Position Fretboards
  Simplify Spelling
✓ Substitute Symbols
  Edit Learned Chords...
  Change Chord Suffix Fonts...
```

Figure 5-21(A)

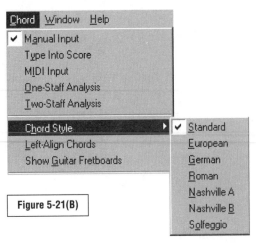

chord symbol into the score. Click again on only one of the chord's notes for which you want a chord symbol to appear.

Chord Styles

Finale offers several alternate ways to create and view chord symbols in your score. These options are great for the educator, studio arranger, and nonprofessional desk top music enthusiast.

To change chord styles, simply go to the Chord pull-down menu and select the Chord Style command. Figure 5-21(B)

To change chord styles simply select a style and the chords style will automatically update. Figure 5-21(C) illustrates the applications of the various Chord Styles.

Figure 5-21(B)

Figure 5-21(C)

5-G Using One-Staff Analysis

1. Try the technique above after creating a new file for the example in Figure 5-22.

Figure 5-22

Two-Staff Analysis

If you want Finale to analyze a chord that's notated on two staves, choose Two-Staff Analysis from the Chord menu; then click the notes in the upper staff. Finale analyzes all the notes in both staves, and places a chord symbol into the score. (This is a useful option when you are adding chord symbols to piano music.) Click again at each place you want a chord symbol to appear.

5-H Using Two-Staff Analysis

1. Try the technique above after creating a new file for the example in Figure 5-23.

Figure 5-23

Hint: Use Mirror Tool for both layers in the first measure

Moving and Deleting Chord Symbols

- Click on the Chord Tool CM7.

- Click on the staff containing the chord symbols. Four small arrows will appear at the left edge of the screen. These arrows control the baseline for the chord symbols—the line against which the bottoms of the chord symbols align. (Make sure Position Chords is selected in the Chord menu.)

- To move more than one chord symbol, drag the positioning arrows up or down in the following four ways:

  Drag the first (far left) triangle up or down to move all the chords in the piece.

  Drag the second triangle to move the chords in this staff only, regardless of the position of the far left triangle.

  Drag the third triangle, in Page View, to move the chords in this staff in this system only.

  Dragging the far right triangle does not move any existing chord symbols; instead, it sets the position for the next one you enter.

- If you want to move a single chord symbol, click the note to which it's attached. The chord's handle will appear. Drag the chord's handle to move it. You can also press the arrow keys to "nudge" a chord for fine positioning; select and press the Delete key to remove a chord.

Transposing Chord Symbols

Finale's chord symbols are intelligent enough to transpose automatically when you change the key signature; a Cmaj7 in the key of C will become an Fmaj7 in the key of F.

If you inadvertently enter chord symbols before setting the key signature, however, you can use the following method to transpose the chord symbols independent of the key and the existing music.

- Click the Mass Mover Tool ⊞ and select the region containing the chord symbols that you want to transpose.

- From the Change submenu of the Mass Edit menu, choose **Chord Assignments.** The Change Chord Assignments dialog box will appear.

- Click **Transpose.** The Transposition dialog box will appear.

- Specify the interval by which you want the chord symbols transposed, and click OK. Click OK again.

Copying Chords from One Region to Another

In this section, the source region is the music that currently contains the chords, and the target region is the music to which you want to copy them.

- Click the Mass Mover Tool ⏹. Choose **Move Entry Items** from the Mass Mover menu. The Entry Items dialog box will appear.

- Select Chords. Click OK.

- Select the source region. (See Chapter Four, "Measure Setup/Copying," Figs. 4-16 through 4-20, for some region-selecting shortcuts.)

- Drag the highlighted region so that it's superimposed on the beginning of the target region. If the target passage is off-screen, scroll to it, then, while pressing Option-shift simultaneously, click it.

If you are copying chords horizontally, and Select Partial Measures is turned off in the Mass Mover menu, then the "How many times?" box will appear. Specify the number of times you want the chords copied, and click OK.

Finale only places chords on notes that fall on the same beats as they did in the source measures. The chords will automatically transpose if the source and target passages are in different keys.

Programming a Chord Symbol Metatool

You can assign a complete chord symbol to each of the number keys 1 through 8 on your Macintosh keyboard, for use as described below.

- Click on the Chord Tool CM7. While pressing Option, press a number key (1 through 8). The Chord Definition box will appear.

- Define the chord. See pp. 158–164 for full instructions on creating chord symbols.

- Click OK (or press Return). When you return to the score, it will appear as though nothing has happened. In fact, you have prepared Finale to enter the chord you just described whenever you use the Metatool (see below).

- Click on the Chord Tool CM7.

- While pressing the number key (1 through 8) corresponding to the desired Metatool, click a note or rest. The chord symbol will appear. Using this method, you can rapidly click fully formed chord symbols into your score. (You still cannot enter a chord symbol over a default whole rest.)

Fretboard Diagrams

The five-line staff is used by all classical and jazz instruments, but some stringed instruments, such as the guitar, banjo, and electric bass, use fretboard diagrams in addition. These instruments can also read from diagrams of the fingerboard and the finger position on the frets and strings of the instrument.

- Open up the "Bill Bailey Excerpt" or create the example in Figure 5-24.
- Click on the Chord Tool CM7 . The Chord menu will appear.
- Create the musical example in Figure 5-24 with lyrics and chords.

Figure 5-24

Entering Fretboard Diagrams

- Choose **Show Guitar Fretboards** from the Chord menu. Since you have already added chord symbols to your piece, the guitar diagrams will now appear (see Figure 5-25). If you have not yet added chord symbols, enter them now. As you add each chord name, its fretboard diagram will appear.

Figure 5-25

Removing Fretboard Diagrams

- Click on the Chord Tool, and choose Show Guitar Fretboard Diagrams. The diagrams will toggle and disappear. There should no longer be a check mark next to Show Guitar Fretboards in the Chord menu.

Moving Fretboard Diagrams

- Click on the Chord tool. The Chord menu will appear, and four small triangles will appear at the left edge of the screen.

- Select Show Guitar Fretboards from the Chord menu. The Fretboards will reappear.

- Choose Position Fretboards from the Chord menu. You have just told Finale that the triangles should adjust the baseline for the diagrams instead of the chord symbols.

- Drag the triangle handles up or down. The far left triangle is used to set the baseline for the entire piece.

Chapter Five Review

Using the Lyric and Chord Tools in Chapter Five, you now know how to create lyrics, chord symbols, and guitar fretboard diagrams, as well as:

Analysis of chords in one or two staves

How to create a lead sheet

How to edit lyrics

How to use automatic and manual chord symbol entry

Chapter Five Project

Open a new document and save as "Project 5-1," or work with your existing '"Bill Bailey Excerpt." Create the following score by entering the following lead sheet example, adding lyrics, chords, and guitar fretboards.

Bill Bailey, Won't You Please Come Home?

Words & Music by Hughie Cannon

CHAPTER SIX

The Final Score

In this chapter, you will enter a multiple-stave score and learn to prepare a score and then extract parts for final layout and printing.

6-A Entering the Score "Bach Chorale"

1. Use the Setup Wizard to create the four staves for the "Bach Chorale" Enter the following Bach musical example in Figure 6-1. Be sure to name the staves in the Edit Staff Attributes To; fermatas are created with the Articulation Tool.

Layout and Printing

The final step in creating a score is the output stage, where you "tweak" your score to print it out in exactly the way you desire. Before you work with the Page Layout Tool, you should always use the Apply Beat or Note Spacing in the Mass Edit menu.

The Apply Beat Spacing and Apply Note Spacing commands (in the Music Spacing submenu, Figure 6-2[A]) lay out the notes of each measure in a slightly different fashion.

With Beat Spacing, Finale calculates where each beat should be positioned in the measure. Any notes within the beat are spaced linearly (where an eighth note gets exactly half as much space as a quarter note, etc.).

Bach Chorale

Figure 6-1

With Note Spacing, Finale consults the allotment settings to determine the precise position of every single note or rest in a measure. Thus, Note Spacing provides more exact spacing than does Beat Spacing.

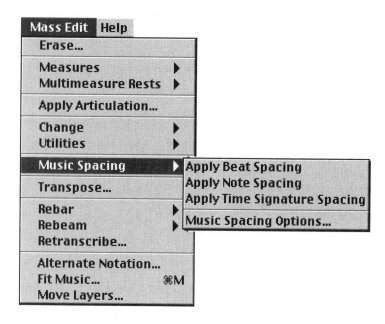

Figure 6-2(A)

It is possible to freely mix and match applications of the two spacing commands within a piece.

Working With the Page Layout Tool

1. Define the measurement units for your score. Select Measurement Units from the Options pull-down menu in the main menu. Choose inches if it is not already selected. This will define the measurements that Finale displays as inches globally. Other options are also available (see Figure 6-2[B]).

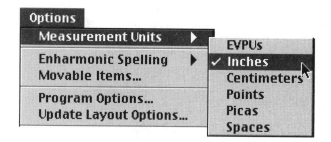

Figure 6-2(B)

2. Finale has two features, rulers and grids that help with the final stages of laying out elements in a score. Both of these options can be found in the View pull-down menu and may be turned on or off the screen by selecting the command again.

Figure 6-2(C)

Figure 6-2(D)

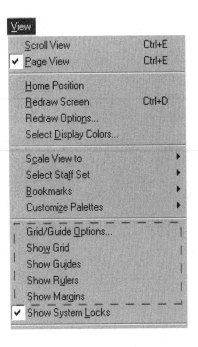

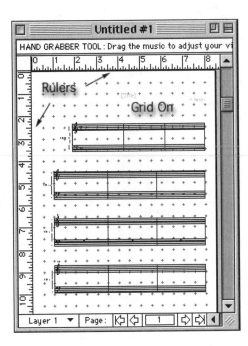

3. Rulers are straightforward with cursor movements appearing as lines on both the horizontal and vertical screen rulers. These visual aids can help when you are dragging a score item's handle or graphic component to a new location.

4. Grids allow you to place user-defined grid markings on the screen to assist with page layout. You can select the color, spacing between grid makings and style (solid, dashes, dots and crosshairs) by selecting the Grid/Guide Options from the View menu's pull-down menu.

Figure 6-2(E)

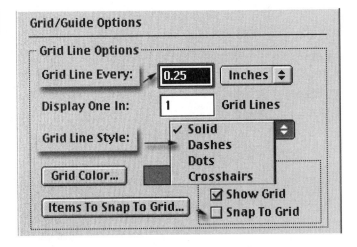

5. The Items To Snap To Grid will allow items with a check to align with your grid setting when released. This option will take effect when the Snap To Grid box is checked. The all or none buttons allow you to quickly select or deselect items.

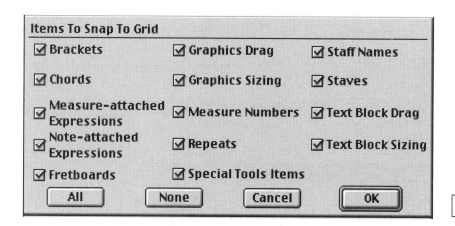

Figure 6-2(F)

Keep in mind that these options can be viewed or active as needed and can be a big help for score layout.

Viewing the Layout

You will remember from Chapter One that Finale offers a second view of your music—Page View—where the music is laid out as it will be when you print. Particularly if you plan to work with larger scores, you will find it much quicker to do your editing in Scroll View. The computer can redraw the screen much faster in Scroll View, so reserve Page View for page layout, adding titles, and final proofing before you print.

• Choose Page View from the View menu ⌘-~/Ctrl+E. Finale shows you the full-page layout view of your score. Now reduce the screen display so that you can see the whole page of music at once.

• Choose Scale View To from the View menu; without releasing the mouse button, drag onto the submenu and select Fit in Window ⌘-I/not available in Windows. Finale reduces the music just enough to display the entire page on your monitor.

The Finale Default File provides you with a dummy title, or you can create the title with the Setup Wizard; the first system has been moved down from the top of the page to make room for it.

Notice that the measures are not evenly spaced in Page View, even though they looked fine in Scroll View. Look at the bottom system, for example; notice that the last two measures stretch across the entire last system.

Page Size

- Double-click the **Page Layout Tool** 🗋 . The dialog box in Figure 6-3 will appear.

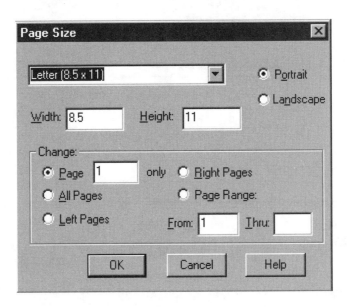

Figure 6-3

- To make an adjustment to the page's size, select the Page Size command from the Page Layout Menu.

The following dialog box will appear, allowing you to set up your page requirements for the score. The fly-out triangle allows you to select typical page sizes. You can also input custom page settings in the Width and Height fields. Portrait or Landscape orientation can be selected in this dialog box, as well as the range of the score that page resizing will affect.

When you readjust these settings, make sure that you reflect the changes to page size with Page Setup in the File menu (Figure 6-4). It is very important that the page dimensions set with the Page Layout Tool are set to the same page size (letter or legal) for printing (Figure 6-5).

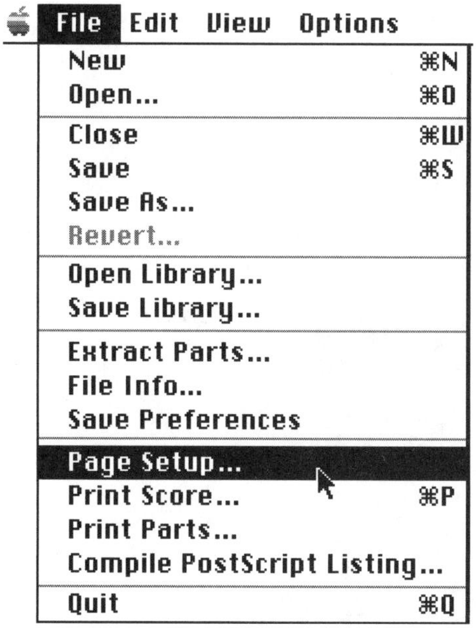

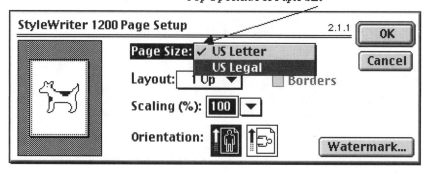

Figure 6-4

Figure 6-5

Look at the last line of music. If your monitor is too small for the entire page to fit, drag the scroll box in the vertical scroll bar all the way to the bottom.

The view percentage commands ⌘-I/Ctrl+I will alter the viewing size only of each page of your document for tweaking.

Figure 6-6

The Previous and Next arrows allow you to view each individual page in your score. The score page number that you are working on will be present in the **Page:** 1 field.

Page Margins

- Select the Page Layout pulldown menu. Select Page Margins from the Page Layout pulldown menu and then Edit Page Margins from the flyout triangle. The dialog box in Figure 6-7 will appear.

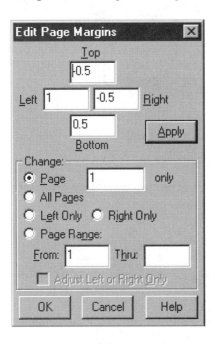

Figure 6-7

The page margin dialog box controls the way music will fill the score's pages. This is an important setting because if it is set to large your printer will not be able to print the outside area of your score.

You control the area by the numbers you place in the four fields Top and Right (use negative numbers only) and Bottom and Left (use positive numbers only). Once you change these settings and click on **Apply**, your score will update. See Figure 6-8.

The change area controls the page range that your settings will affect, such as: all pages, left or right only, or a specified range.

If your score is to be spiral bound, you may want to set page margins that create additional space or a gutter on the left- or right-hand side before final output. This will make sure your score is readable when bound.

Staff Systems

When you select a Staff System handle, you can adjust the spacing of your staves either individually or globally. Use the Systems command in the Page Layout pull-down menu to determine how systems will be adjusted. A check beside the Adjust Current Staff System Only will permit you to only move one system in the Page Layout dialog box. A check beside the Adjust All Staff Systems will allow global adjustment of all systems in the score. By selecting one of the two options you can tweak the score to your personal demands (see Figure 6-9).

Each system will have a consecutive number. This is a good way to catch any printing problems that may occur with your score. When you look through the pages of your score, you may see two of the same system numbers or a skipped number. Go to the **Update Layout** command in the Edit pull-down menu of the main menu ⌘-\ or Ctrl+U in Windows (see Figure 6-8).

You can also use a function called Optimize All Staff Systems command that will remove any instrument from the score that is tacit only for the time it rests from the Page Layout pull-down menu.

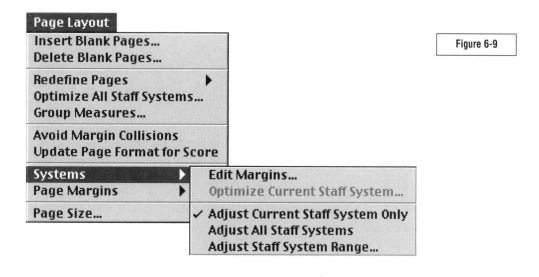

Figure 6-8

Figure 6-9

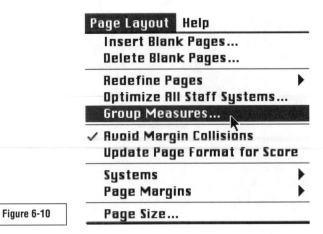

Figure 6-10

Another important command in the Page Layout menu is the **Group Measures** command (see Figure 6-10). When you select this command, a dialog box will appear for defining how many measures will be in a system (see Figure 6-11).

Figure 6-11

This is the first step in massaging the score and will determine the number of measures per line of music globally.

You must decide how much space you will need for your score. If lyrics will be present, you may not be able to fit as many measures per line. Be objective as to how crammed you want the music to look or the length of the score when using this tool.

After selecting the Group Measures command, the Mass Measure Grouping dialog box (Figure 6-12) will appear, and you can simply set a number
in the Freeze Layout field to specify how many measures will be on a line for
the entire score.

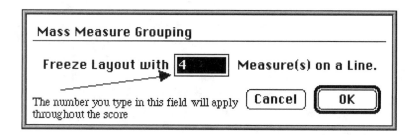

Figure 6-12

In the Page Layout View, you have the following options for designing
your page layout:

Staff system height and width adjustments

Spacing between Staff Systems

The number of staves on a page

Figures 6-13 through 6-15 show you how to accomplish these
adjustments.

As you make an adjustment, you will see it upgraded on the computer
screen. By repositioning and spacing you can control the number of
systems per page.

Always use the Update Layout command to make sure the measures,
numbers, spacing, etc., are correct before attempting any new changes.

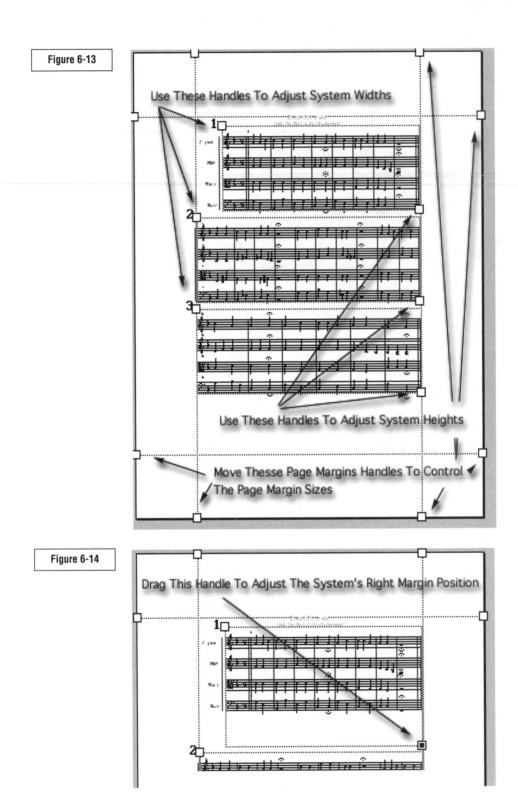

Figure 6-13

Use These Handles To Adjust System Widths

Use These Handles To Adjust System Heights

Move Thesse Page Margins Handles To Control The Page Margin Sizes

Figure 6-14

Drag This Handle To Adjust The System's Right Margin Position

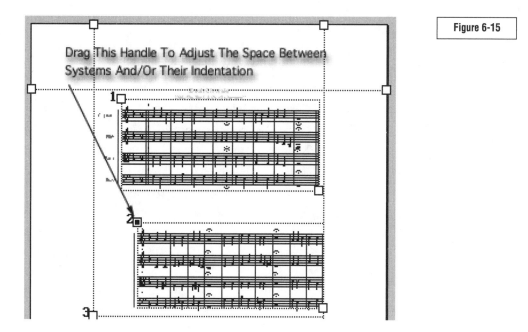

Figure 6-15

Optimizing a System of Staves

Optimizing will make all staves in Staff Systems independently adjustable. Optimizing also removes empty staves from the Staff Systems in page view when the instrument(s) are tacet in the score.

When you Select the Optimize All Staff Systems command from the Page Layout pull-down menu, the following dialog box will appear (Figure 6-16), which allows you to define its operation.

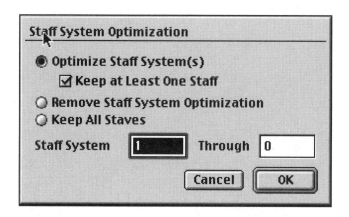

Figure 6-16

If you select the Show Music option, whatever page you are working on will display a reduced percentage of the actual music on your screen. This can be selected or deselected at any time.

After tweaking your score, such as using the Update Layout command ⌘-\ or Ctrl+U in Windows, there may be a page with only a measure or two on the final page. There is a quick page-layout trick you can use to pull the last measures back onto the first page.

If your monitor is not large enough to see the first two lines of music, drag the scroll box in the vertical scroll bar upward (or drag with the Hand Grabber) until you can see the first two lines.

Your aim is to put a measure back onto the end of the first system. To do so, you will use a special Finale feature called Fit Music, a function of the Mass Mover Tool 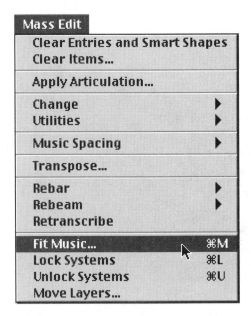.

- Select the Mass Mover Tool.

- Select all the measures you want to be on a single line of music in the page.

- Go to the Mass Edit command in the main menu.

- Select **Fit Music** (see Figure 6-19[A]) or use the power key macro ⌘-**M**/Ctrl+M.

Figure 6-19(A)

Mass Edit	
Clear Entries and Smart Shapes	
Clear Items...	
Apply Articulation...	
Change	▶
Utilities	▶
Music Spacing	▶
Transpose...	
Rebar	▶
Rebeam	▶
Retranscribe	
Fit Music...	⌘M
Lock Systems	⌘L
Unlock Systems	⌘U
Move Layers...	

- Choose the radio button Fit Selected Measures Into One System and click OK (see Figure 6-19[B]). All selected measures are now on one line.

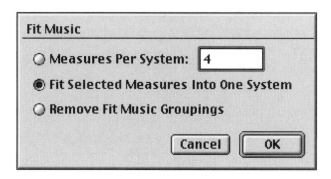

Figure 6-19(B)

When you have used the **Fit Music** command, small **System Locks** are placed in the score. If you find them a distraction you have the option to show or hide them. The System Lock icons indicate which staff systems are "locked" against reflowing when performing an Update Layout command (unless you have selected Remove Fit Measure Groupings). Systems are locked when you use the Fit Music command in the Mass Edit menu and when you move measures using the up or down arrow keys. Use Command–L/not available in Windows and Command–U/ not available in Windows commands to Lock and Unlock selected systems when in Mass Mover.

To hide the System Locks, choose the Hide System Locks or Show System Locks command in the View pull-down menu.

When the Mass Mover Tool is selected, you simply select a measure in page view and can move these measure(s) up or down a system by simply hitting the up or down arrow keys, respectively.

Figure 6-19(C)

Updating the Measure Layout

▶ *Because you will always need to update the measure layout before you print or after you make page layout changes, you may want to remember the keyboard equivalent for Update Layout: ⌘-\ (or Ctrl+U; the backslash is under the Delete key).*

Be aware that a measure that looks cluttered in Scroll View may look correct in Page View.

When you used the Music Spacing command, you corrected the spacing of the notes, lyrics, and accidentals of your piece; however, Finale has not yet recalculated the effects of your respacing on the layout of the measures. To speed up the program, Finale puts off music spacing until you specify it.

• Choose Update Layout from the Edit menu.

Measures will neatly respace and be justified so that they are flush with the margins of the page. This will also reorganize the measure and system numbers correctly.

You will also notice, however, that the music now fits on only four *systems* (lines of music). The score would look better if the systems were evenly spaced on the page from top to bottom, instead of being tightly spaced in the middle of the page. Also, you may decide to indent the first system. You can make these formatting changes using the Page Layout Tool.

If your monitor is not large enough to see the first two lines of music, drag the scroll box in the vertical scroll bar upward (or drag with the Hand Grabber) until you can see the first two lines.

Moving a Measure to a Different Line in Page View

• Click on the Mass Mover Tool, and click on any measure you wish to move to a system either above or below. You can tell Finale to push the selected measure into the system above it.

• Press the ⬆ key. When you select a measure and press ⬆ or ⬇, Finale pushes that measure onto the system above or below its current system, respectively.

When you move a measure, Finale adjusts all the measures on the page.

Creating a Title (The Text Block Tool)

A "title" is any single line of text on a page. Titles, subtitles, composer credits, page numbers, copyright notices, and dates are possible examples.

- First we want to change the dummy title to "Bach Chorale"; then we'll add the subtitle "Help Us, Lord, in Our Endeavors."

- From the View menu, choose Home Position. In Page View, Home Position shifts the view to the upper-left corner of the page on which you are working. In Scroll View, it returns you to measure 1. You can also use the ⌘-H/Home key keyboard shortcut.

- Select the **Text Block Tool** from the Main Tool Palette . Two new menu items will appear in the main menu: Text and Frame. The Text menu is where you select the text parameters, such as font, style, justification, etc. (see Figure 6-20 [A]).

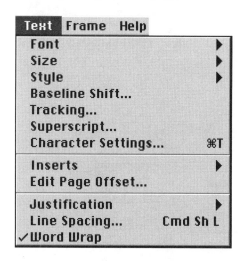

Figure 6-20(A)

- The dummy title ("Title") in the score now contains a handle. To edit a title, double-click its handle. This will place a dotted box around the title, and if you click and drag across the dummy title and type, you will replace it with the title of your score. Enter the title "Bach Chorale."

Alignment and other text page options can be changed by selecting a text block's handle and then using the Frame menu's pull-down command Attributes ⌘-Shift-T/Ctrl+Shift+T in the main menu (see Figure 6-20 [B]).

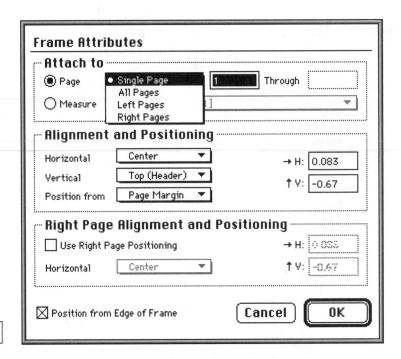

Figure 6-20(B)

Alignment and text attachment are controlled from the Alignment and Positioning flyouts in Figure 6-21.

Figure 6-21

- Make sure that the Attach To option is set to Single Page for your title. It is very important that you select Single Page if it is a title or subtitle, so that all the other pages of a score do not have the title or subtitle present.

- If you want to change the typeface, click the Text pull-down menu in the main menu and go to the Font command. Use the submenu to the right to pick the desired font (the dummy title is in 18-point Times).

Adding a Subtitle

- Double-click just below the title. (The subtitle will appear at the vertical location of your click.) Type "Help Us, Lord, in Our Endeavors." (The dummy subtitle is in 12-point Times italic.)

- From the Frame menu's pull-down command Attributes, select "Single Page." Choose your Alignment and Positioning options ("Center," "Page Margin") if not already selected.

- Set the font and size from the Text pull-down menu in the main menu. For a subtitle, a 12- or 14-point size should work well. Use the same font you used for the title.

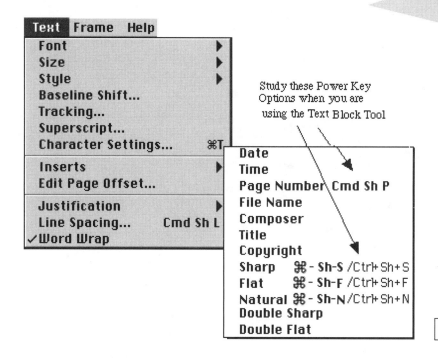

Study these Power Key Options when you are using the Text Block Tool

Keep in mind that you can use these Text Block techniques to add any type of text information to a score, including page numbers and a copyright symbol. Use Inserts from the Text pull-down menu to create insert options (see Figure 6-22).

Figure 6-22

Creating Parts from a Score

One of the best features of any notation program is the ability to create a single score and then have the notation software create all the parts automatically. The simplest method available for printing parts is to choose

Print Parts from the File menu. This method will not give any individual formatting, and the measure widths in the score are retained in the individual parts. When you choose the Print Parts command from the file menu, simply click OK in the two following dialog boxes.

Extract Parts

A much more precise way is to use the **Extract Parts** command from the File menu. With this method, an Extract Parts dialog box appears, asking you for information as to the appearance of the new documents (see Figure 6-23). Highlight the staves you want extracted from your score in the Staves field. These staves will be saved as individual files, one for each part. The File Names radio buttons generate names from the "Bach Chorale" title of the original document.

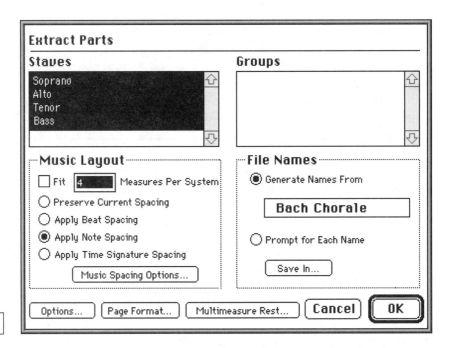

Figure 6-23

You can select your music layout, such as the number of measures per system, Beat Spacing, or Note Spacing as desired. When you click on OK, the following status box appears, and will change to show you the status of Finale while it is executing the Extract Parts command (see Figure 6-24).

Figure 6-24

Extracting Parts

Current: [Staff 3]
Status: Laying Out Entries

Click Mouse Button or
Type Command "." to Cancel

Each part will be saved as a new Finale file, which you can "tweak" to create the optimal page layout for each part (such as avoiding awkward page turns, etc.). After this command is complete, it may take a few minutes. Each part can be modified and saved before being printed.

Printing Basics

Creating a Landscape or Portrait Score

When working with computer output to printer there are two terms of which you should be aware: *portrait* and *landscape.* These terms refer to the direction your printer will use when printing a score.

Portrait is 8.5 x 11 inches in dimension:

Landscape is 11 x 8.5 inches
in dimension for letter-size paper:

I find it very helpful to create Landscape output for scores and Portrait for parts (see Figures 6-25 and 6-26).

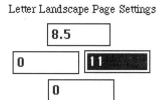

Letter Landscape Page Settings

8.5

0   11

0

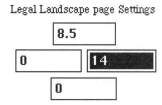

Legal Landscape page Settings

8.5

0   14

0

Figure 6-25

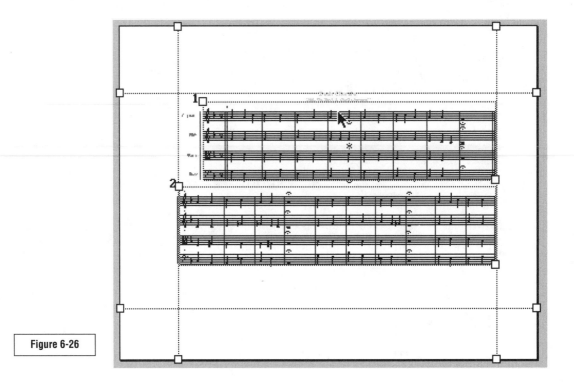

Figure 6-26

Make sure that you select the Landscape printer orientation in Page
Setup under the File menu (see Figure 6-27).

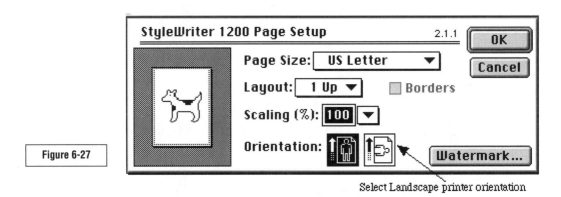

Figure 6-27

Select Landscape printer orientation

Printing

- Choose **Print Score** from the File menu, and click OK in the dialog box
  that appears. In a moment, your printer should begin to print your score.

There are essentially two kinds of printers that work with Finale. Post-Script-equipped printers, such as the LaserWriter series, are suitable for professional publishing. Non-PostScript printers include dot-matrix and inkjet printers—the ImageWriter, DeskWriter, and StyleWriter are some examples. In all cases, be sure you have prepared your Macintosh or Windows setup for printing from Finale.

Chapter Six Review

Using the Page Layout and Text block tools in Chapter Six, you should understand how to create a finished desktop manuscript as well as:

How to create parts from a score

How to create titles

How to reposition staves on each page

Review the material if you do not understand any of the above.

Notes:

Chapter Six Projects

1. Prepare the "Bach Chorale" as a score. Pay attention to margins, spacing, staff names, and overall layout of the piece.

   Hint: Notice that the lower staves do not have measure numbers showing.
   Print out the score.
   Review Staff Tool.

2. Extract the staves of the "Chorale" as separate parts. Open and name each file; then set up each part for layout and printing. Print out the parts.

CHAPTER SEVEN

Special Guitar Notation

Creating Guitar Tablature

Finale can easily create standard tablature for guitar. *Tablature* is a special type of guitar notation where an additional staff is used that contains six lines, representing the six strings of the guitar. The bottom tablature line represents the sixth string; the top line depicts the first string. Here is a great way to remember what number corresponds to each string: *"little number equals little string."* With tablature, small numbers are placed on these lines to illustrate fret numbers in place of noteheads. These fret numbers show where you finger a stringed instrument to play the pitch in the traditional staff (see Figure 7-1[A]). With Finale's tablature functions you can even have rhythm stems applied to the fret/string matrix. (See Figure 7-1[B]).

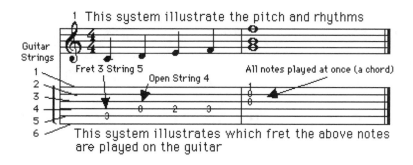

Figure 7-1(A)

Figure 7-1(B)

In Finale each line of tablature is similar to an individual staff. Be careful that you do not accidentally drag or delete one.

Automatic Tablature

The easiest way to create a score incorporating tablature is to use the **Automatic Tablature** command in the **Plug In** pull-down menu. This command works in conjunction with the Mass Mover Tool ⊞.

- Create a new Finale document and input the notes in Figure 7-2.

Figure 7-2

- Select the Mass Mover Tool and highlight all four measures.

- Go to **Plug In** in the main menu and select the Automatic Tablature command (see Figure 7-3). This feature in Finale 97 allows you to automatically create guitar, banjo, electric bass, or tablature for any stringed instrument.

Figure 7-3

- The Automatic Tablature dialog box will appear; make sure that it is set to Guitar in its pop-up menu (Figure 7-4).

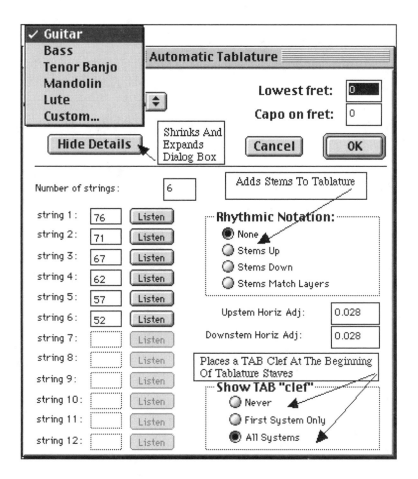

Figure 7-4

The Lowest Fret field determines the position that notes are to be played on the guitar neck. A position is determined by which fret you place the first finger of your left hand. By placing a 5 in the Lowest Fret field, your tablature would reflect where to play the notes in this position. The Capo on Fret would reflect how the music would need to be played if a capo were placed on the guitar's neck. A capo is used to easily transpose a song or for a special effect. It is clipped onto the guitar neck to shorten the strings and allow the guitarist to use the same fingerings in a new key.

• Make sure that all settings in the Automatic Tablature dialog box match Figure 7-4, then select OK . Your score should look like Figure 7-5.

Figure 7-5

- Now let's place this example in the fifth position. Select the Staff Tool and all six lines in Tablature. Press Delete so we can place it in the fifth position (see Figure 7-6).

Figure 7-6

It is a good idea to make sure that you have set the position correctly in the Lowest Fret field. Try the position you will set on the instrument. Finale will let you know if there is a problem with your position setting, or if the number of notes exceeds playability on the instrument, such as the prompts in Figure 7-7.

Figure 7-7

You do not have to create tablature for the entire score at one time. You can use the Mass Mover Tool to select several measures at one time for Automatic Tablature. Each time you create Automatic Tablature you will get a new tablature system, such as in Figure 7-8. You can then use the Mass Mover Tool to copy and paste multiple tablature into a single tablature (tab for short).

Figure 7-8

Automatic Tablature is a wonderful addition to Finale and very easy to use, but it is not infallible. You should always examine and perform all automatic tablature calculations on your guitar. The following instructions will show you how to create tablature from a Tablature Template, which is included in the General Templates Folder; the same technique allows you to correct or update Automatic Tablature inaccuracies.

Creating Tablature from a Template

Another simple way to create a score incorporating tablature is to open the pre-existing Guitar Tablature Template, which is in Finale's Templates folder. Always be sure to do a Save As in the File menu after a template is opened, with the name you intend to use. This will allow the template to remain a template, without any added notes, key or time signatures, etc.

- Select the Open command in the File menu, and go to the Finale folder in your drive. Select the folder that contains Templates, then select the folder that contains General Templates, and finally select Guitar Tablature (see Figure 7-9).

- Go to the File menu and select New.

- When the open dialog box appears, select General Templates.

- Click on Guitar Tablature and select Open.

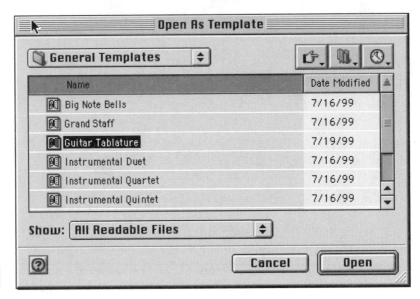

Figure 7-9

This will open the selected document as an Untitled Finale file, protecting the original template from being changed.

- Select Save and name this document "Tablature Example."

- Create the notation shown in Figure 7-10 in the top staff. Always begin creating a Finale tablature document by first placing traditional notation in the upper staff system. If you have Staff Expressions chords or any additional entries in the traditional staff, they will also appear in the tablature system when moved. Therefore, always make sure you move the notes to tablature after you have completed pitch entry, but before any articulations, chords, etc. are placed in the score.

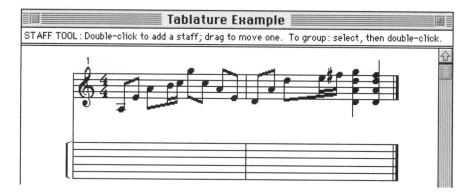

Figure 7-10

- In order to copy notes from the top staff to the tablature staff, select the **Note Mover Tool** ![icon] from the tool palette. When this tool is selected, handles will appear at each note within the selected measure. See Figure 7-11.

Figure 7-11

You must be careful when moving the notes from the upper staff to the tablature staff! Finale thinks of each line in tablature as a separate one-line staff to create tablature; therefore, you must drag all the notes that are on a string together for the entire measure (see Figure 7-12). By holding down the Shift key you can select notes that are at different locations in the measure.

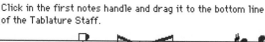
Click in the first notes handle and drag it to the bottom line of the Tablature Staff.

Figure 7-12

A (0) will appear on the fifth line to alert the guitarist performing the piece to play an open fifth string.

You must study any measure for which you will be creating tablature in order to be aware of what pitches in the measure lie on the same string. You must be sure to drag these pitches at the same time. You can simply use the marquee technique or Shift-click to move these pitches together (see Figures 7-13 and 7-14). If you do not use this technique, you will erase any tablature fret number you have already placed on the same string.

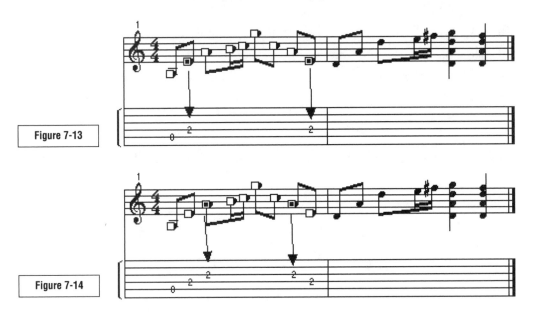

Figure 7-13

Figure 7-14

- Continue using the Note Mover Tool. Shift-click the two sixteenth notes and the non-adjacent C eighth note. Since they will all be placed on the same string, drag them to string two (see Figure 7-15).

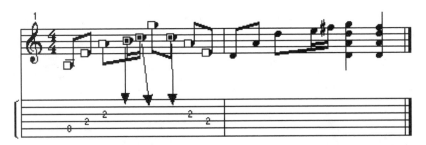

Figure 7-15

Even though measure 2 has chords with each note on different strings, you must drag all notes in a measure played on the same string at the same time (see Figures 7-16 through 7-19). If you make a mistake, you can select the string with the Mass Mover Tool  and press the Clear button in the numerical keypad to erase that string's fret position.

Figure 7-16

Figure 7-17

Figure 7-18

Figure 7-19

Creating Fingerings

Guitar or piano fingerings can be added to any score by using the **Staff Expression Tool** $\boxed{\substack{\text{O} \\ \textit{mf}}}$ in the tool palette and creating a numbering system. You can also create Metatools for fingerings. It is easiest to have your fingerings correspond to the number keys in the alphanumeric keyboard.

Your example should now look like Figure 7-20.

Figure 7-20

- Select the Staff Expression Tool and click on the first note in measure 1. The dialog box in 7-21 will appear. Follow the instructions in Figures 7-21 through 7-23 to create your fingerings.

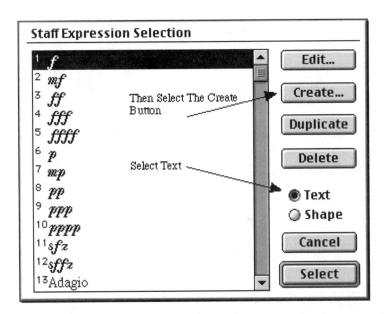

Figure 7-21

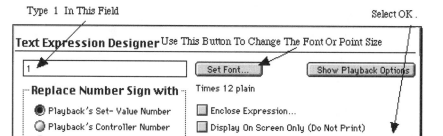

Type 1 In This Field   Select OK.

Text Expression Designer Use This Button To Change The Font Or Point Size

1

Set Font...   Show Playback Options

Replace Number Sign with   Times 12 plain

- Playback's Set- Value Number   ☐ Enclose Expression...
- Playback's Controller Number   ☐ Display On Screen Only (Do Not Print)
- Playback's Pass Number

Cancel   OK

Figure 7-22

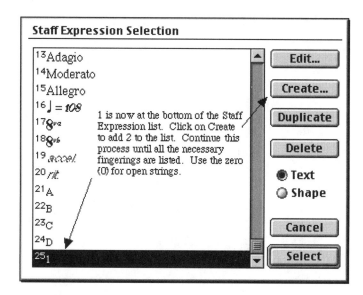

Staff Expression Selection

¹³Adagio	Edit...
¹⁴Moderato	Create...
¹⁵Allegro	
¹⁶♩ = *108*	Duplicate
¹⁷8ᵛᵃ	
¹⁸8ᵛᵇ	Delete
¹⁹ accel	
²⁰rit.	● Text
²¹A	○ Shape
²²B	
²³C	Cancel
²⁴D	
²⁵1	Select

1 is now at the bottom of the Staff Expression list. Click on Create to add 2 to the list. Continue this process until all the necessary fingerings are listed. Use the zero (0) for open strings.

Figure 7-23

- Once all the required fingerings have been created, press the Select button. Simply OK the next dialog box (Figure 7-24) and drag your fingering to the desired position in your score.

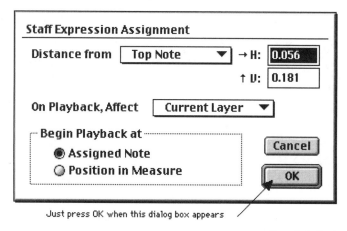

Staff Expression Assignment

Distance from Top Note ▼ → H: 0.056
                                  ↑ U: 0.181

On Playback, Affect Current Layer ▼

Begin Playback at
● **Assigned Note**   Cancel
○ **Position in Measure**   OK

Just press OK when this dialog box appears

Figure 7-24

- After this fingering is in place, create Metatools (Shift key and a 1-9 or A-Z to program) for all the fingering numbers, and click to enter them into the score.

- Add the fingerings in Figure 7-25 to your guitar tablature example.

As a rule, always add fingerings after you have created the tab-lature staff. This will prevent having to delete fingering numbers from the fret numbers in tablature.

Figure 7-25

Have a guitarist play through your score to make sure it is correct before you add articulations, chords, fingerings, etc. Find some printed examples and practice creating them in Finale to increase your facility with this technique.

Creating Custom Fingerboards

While the Seville font (included with Finale) provides many standard fingerboards (chord diagrams), many complex fingerboards are not included. You can create custom fingerboards and then use the Staff Expression Tool 𝄞 to add them to your score. The following method will allow you to create custom fingerboards within Finale, using Finale's Shape Designer, a built-in, easy-to-use graphics program that is similar to other drawing programs such as Super Paint, Claris Paint, or Mac Draw.

- Create only the notes and key signature for the musical example in Figure 7-26.

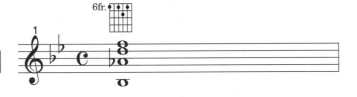

Figure 7-26

Entering the Shape Designer

- Click on the Staff Expression Tool and click a note entry on the staff.

- Click Shape (Figure 7-27).

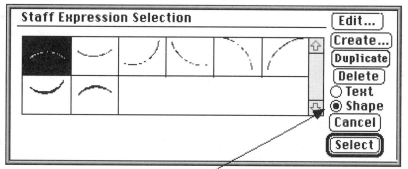

Make sure that shape is selected

Figure 7-27

- Click Create (Figure 7-28).

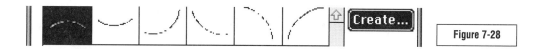

Figure 7-28

The dialog box in Figure 7-29 will appear.

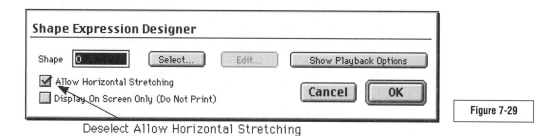

Deselect Allow Horizontal Stretching

Figure 7-29

- Always deselect the Allow Horizontal Stretching box, especially since it is on as a default in the Shape Designer. This will maintain the finger dots on the proper string when placing them into the score.

- Click the Select button (Figure 7-30).

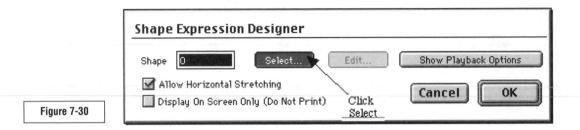

Figure 7-30

The dialog box in Figure 7-31 will appear.

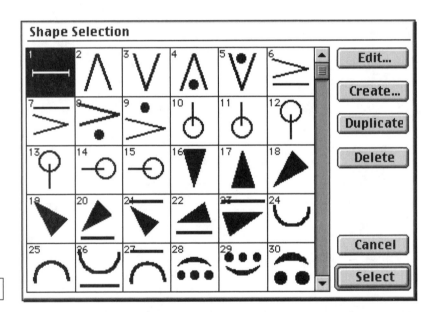

Figure 7-31

- Click the Create button. The Shape Designer will then become available.

Working with the Shape Designer

If you have worked with any type of drawing program, the Shape Designer will be no mystery. You create objects that can be moved and grouped for use in Finale. The tool palette at the top of the window will allow you to create custom fretboards (see Figure 7-32).

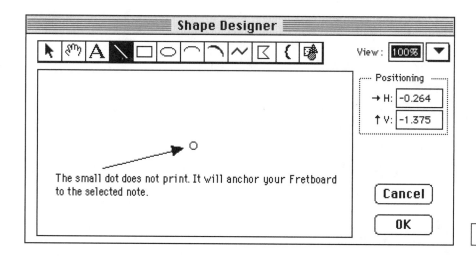

The small dot does not print. It will anchor your Fretboard to the selected note.

Figure 7-32

There are three tools in the Shape Designer palette with which you will work (see Figure 7-33).

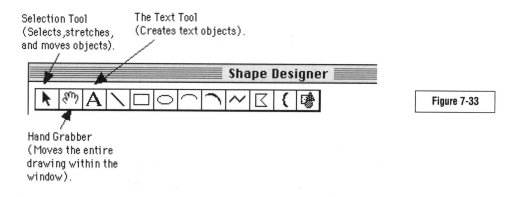

Selection Tool
(Selects, stretches, and moves objects).

The Text Tool
(Creates text objects).

Hand Grabber
(Moves the entire drawing within the window).

Figure 7-33

Creating Fingerboards in the Shape Designer

- Set the View Percentage to 400% so you can position characters more easily. Click View to display the pop-up menu. The View Percentage selector is to the right of the window (see Figure 7-34).

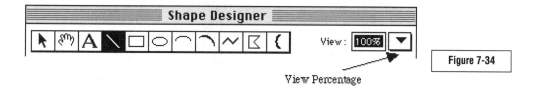

View Percentage

Figure 7-34

25%
50%
75%
100%
200%
400%
800%
View: 400%
Positioning
H: 2.569
V: 1.292

Figure 7-35

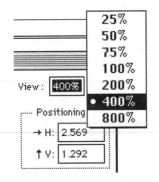

Select 400% and then release the mouse (see Figure 7-35).

Shape Designer
Show
Send to Back ⌘B
Bring to Front ⌘F
Group ⌘G
Ungroup ⌘U
Select Font...

Figure 7-36

Selecting a Font in the Shape Designer

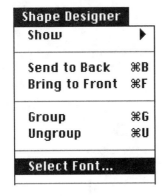

- Go to the Shape Designer pull-down menu. Choose the Select Font command (Figure 7-36).
- Set the font to Seville at a 36-point size (see Figure 7-37).
- Click OK.

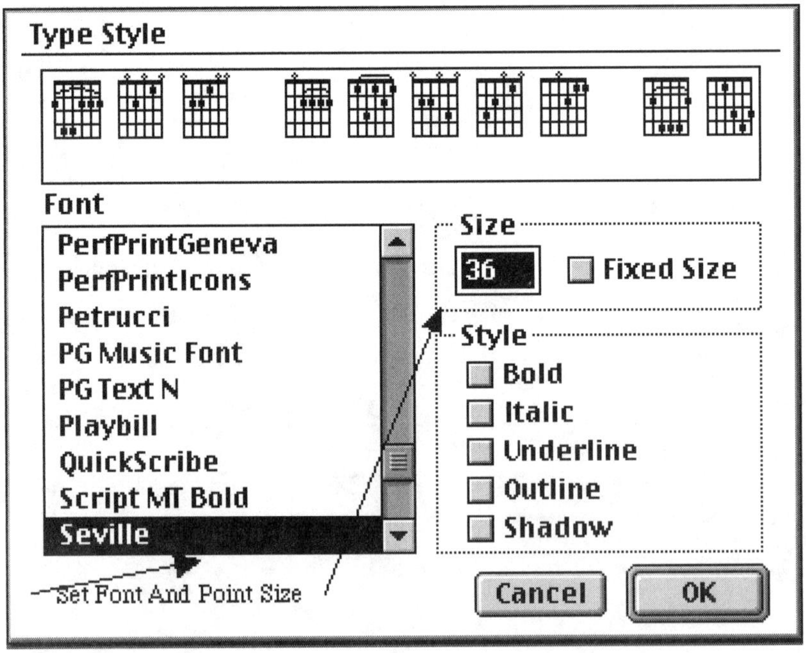

Type Style
Font
PerfPrintGeneva
PerfPrintIcons
Petrucci
PG Music Font
PG Text N
Playbill
QuickScribe
Script MT Bold
Seville
Size
36
Fixed Size
Style
Bold
Italic
Underline
Outline
Shadow
Cancel
OK
Set Font And Point Size

Figure 7-37

Entering an Empty Fingerboard Diagram

- Click on the Text Tool $\boxed{\mathbf{A}}$, and click in the Shape Designer work area.

- Type Shift-zero for the empty fingerboard grid (Figure 7-38).

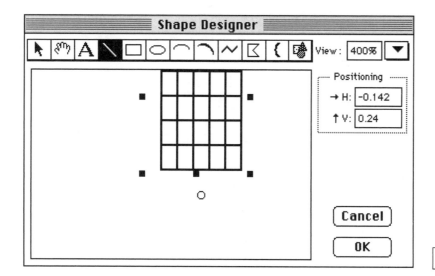

Figure 7-38

- Use the **Selection Tool** $\boxed{\text{\scriptsize ▶}}$ (the first tool in the Shape Designer's palette) to position your fingerboard where you want it.

- The dot on the middle of the Shape Designer work area represents the notehead to which you will attach this fingerboard. Try centering the fingerboard above it with the top part of the guitar frame just touching the top edge of the Shape Designer work area. To do this, use the Selection Tool and drag the frame or any component of the chord fingerboard to its proper position.

Always work with one fingerboard component at a time.

Entering a Fingerboard Character

- Click in the Shape Designer work area where you want the next character to be.

- Click the Text Tool.

- Type the character you want to add (usually the tilde key for the black dot; see Figure 7-39).

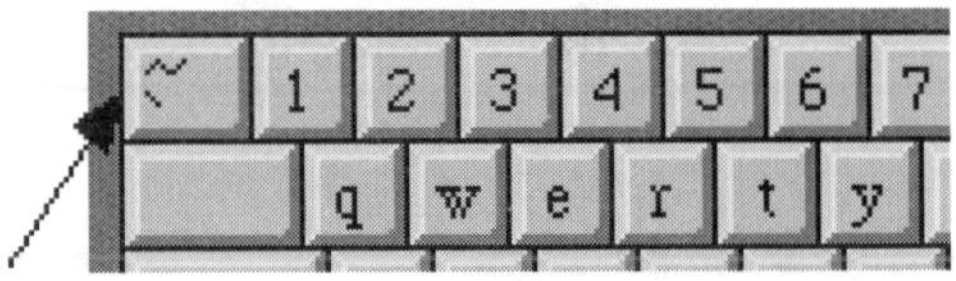

Figure 7-39

- Repeat the steps for this section for each additional fingerboard character you want to add (see Figure 7-40).

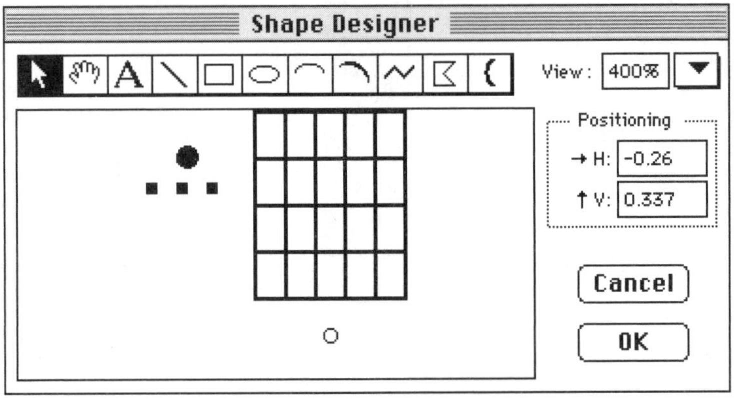

Figure 7-40

- Use the Selection Tool to drag your fretboard components to the desired string. The number keys 1 through [=] will give you position numbers for your fingerboard (see Figure 7-41).

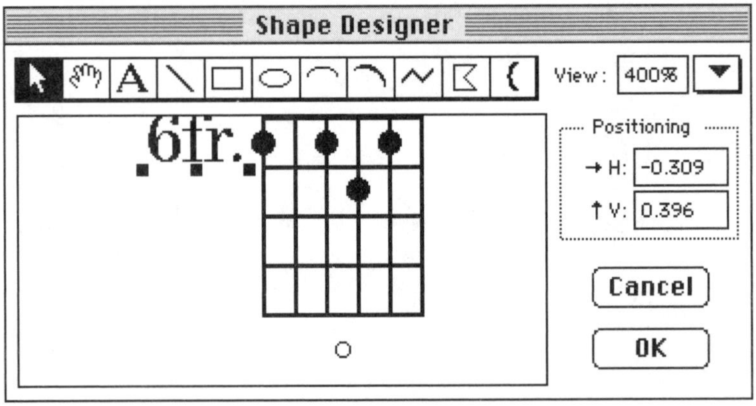

Figure 7-41

- After you have finished making the fingerboard, select all the elements in your fretboard by clicking Select All, ⌘-**A**/Ctrl+**A**. Then select the Group Command from the Shape Designer menu (see Figure 7-42) or use the keyboard shortcut ⌘-**G**.

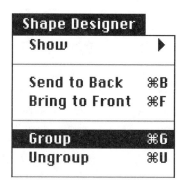

Figure 7-42

With the Group command selected, Finale treats the fingerboard as one shape. Only one positioning handle is displayed on the screen, so you will not accidentally misalign characters in your custom fingerboard. Click OK. In the Shape Selection dialog box, scroll to the end until you see your new fingerboard. Click on it and click Select. Click OK, then Select, then OK in the following dialog boxes.

Your final fretboard diagram should look like Figure 7-43.

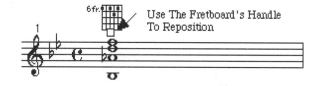

Figure 7-43

To Add More Dots on the Fingerboard

If you need additional dots on the fingerboard (the Shape Designer allows a maximum of 16 instructions), create a Text Expression that is just the dot, and place it on top of the existing fingerboard diagram that is in the score, using the Staff Expression Tool.

- It is a good idea if adding many chord grids to set up a template that has the chord elements already available. If you create a default chord grid that contains the elements in Figure 7-44 you can easily use this Shape as a starting point for your chord design.

Figure 7-44

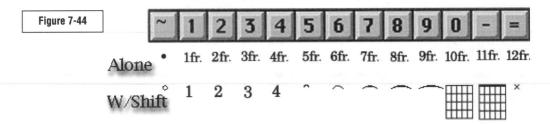

- If you use this technique it is best to make this the first guitar chord grid you create, or keep a journal as to the Shape Expression number for the default. Since you can't zoom in on an Expression Selection dialog box to see what chord quality a number has, it is a good idea to keep a journal that compares the Shape Expression number with the chord quality. This

Figure 7-45

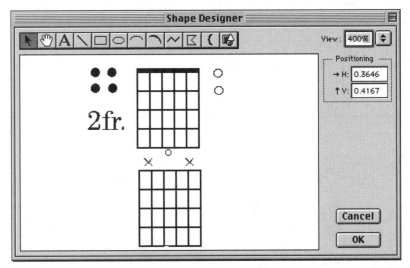

will make it very easy to select a chord(s) that repeatedly appear in your score.

- If you need more frets for a big finger stretch you can superimpose two blank chord grids on top of each other.

- Once you have created the default chord grid you can select it and the Duplicate button. This will make a duplicate Expression Shape. If you select the newly duplicated Expression Shape and the Edit button, the

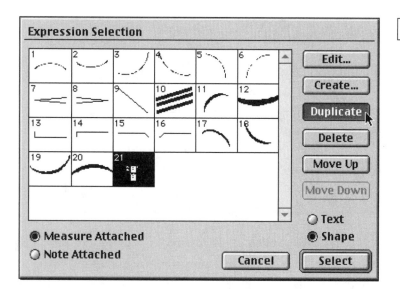

Figure 7-46

Shape Designer Dialog Box will appear. Simply click on an element to reposition it or the Delete/BackSpace key to remove it from the grid.

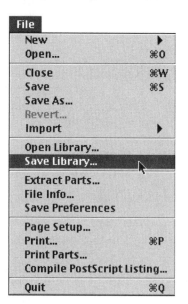

Figure 7-47

- Once you have created a default chord grid or a set of chords you know you will be reusing in other scores, make it a habit to create a Shape Expression Library. When you have finished your score or just created a default Chord Grid, you can save these new Shape Expressions as a Library that can be reloaded into another score before you input score elements.

- To save a library, go to the File's pull-down menu and select the Save Library command. This will bring up the dialog box in figure 7-48.

- The following dialog box appears that allows you to specify the type of library you want to save. Select Shape Expressions, but keep in mind that all of the other elements you create in a score can also be saved as a library (articulations, text expressions, text repeats, etc.).

Figure 7-48

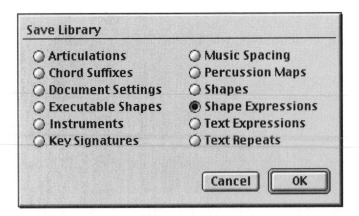

- Once you have selected Shape Expressions and OK, you have a final dialog box that lets you specify a name for your library and where it will be saved. As a rule of thumb, give your library a name that explains the content (Mostly Major Seventh Chords, Default Chord Grid). You should keep this in the Library folder of your Finale 2000 folder.

Figure 7-49

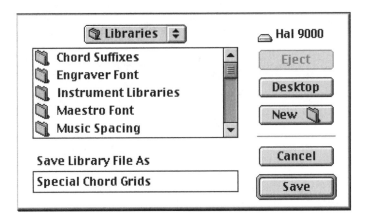

Chapter Seven Review

You now know how to do the following:

Use the shape designer to create custom guitar grids.

Create guitar tablature.

Create/add fingerings.

Chapter Seven Projects

1. Open a new document and save as "Project 7-1." Create the following score using the shape designer.

Hint: Use "Shift" "~" for open strings

Hint: Overlap and offset two Fretboards for big-stretch voicings

2. Open a new document and save as "Project 7-2." Create the following score using a tablative template.

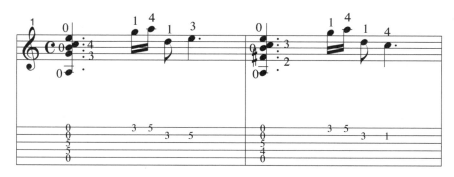

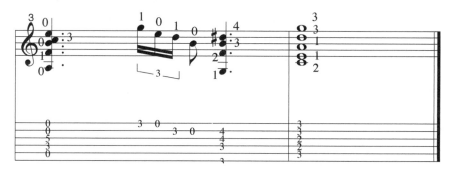

Finale and
Computer Terminology

If this is your first experience with the Macintosh computer platform, you should take some time to learn the basics from a guided tour (usually called Macintosh Basics) to get used to working with a computer mouse. The following important computer terms should be understood or assimilated and will apply to all available computer software.

Active Window: The currently selected window, where the next action will take place. The active window is always on top of all other windows, and its title bar is highlighted.

Alphanumeric Keyboard: An acronym for a computer keyboard that is a combination of letters (alphabet-*alpha*) and numbers (*numeric*) used for computer input.

Application: A computer software program designed to speed up and/or simplify "real world" human tasks such as accounting, word processing, sequencing, music notation, etc.

Chord Suffix: Various numerals that follow the pitch letter and indicate extensions of the chord (sevenths and ninths), added notes, or pitch alterations.

Clicking: By pressing down the mouse button and releasing it, you are signaling the computer that a piece of information is being selected. Selected objects will be highlighted (white will become black), signifying that the object or icon is selected. Shift-clicking will allow you to select more than one icon or object.

Command Key: Used in conjunction with specified characters as a substitute for the mouse. If you look at many of the menu commands, you will see the command symbol to the right followed by a letter or number. Pressing the Command key while typing the letter or number will cause the same results as pulling down the menu and releasing the mouse button.

Contiguous: Items on a computer screen that are immediately next to each other. (See antonym, *Noncontiguous*)

Default: When several options are available with a computer program and you do not pick one, then one is automatically assigned by default. You can also design personal default settings for options when you launch a program.

Default Window: A computer- or user-assigned window that appears when a program is launched.

Delete Key: A computer keyboard key that will backspace, removing a single letter or setting in a dialog box field. If a handle is selected for a number or word in a field, the Delete key will eliminate it from your score.

Desktop: The main Finder screen, consisting of a white menu bar and the gray or colored "desk surface," with the hard drive and trash icons. Objects can be placed on the desk surface, moved about, and removed. It can be thought of as an actual desk.

Dialog Box: A box on the screen requesting information or a decision from you.

Disk Initialization or Formatting: Before a computer can store data on a disk, the disk must be organized into a form that allows data to be stored and retrieved—a type of indexing system. Formatting/ initialization typically involves inserting a blank disk in a disk drive and running a formatting/initialization program. The disk drive will then magnetically mark the disk where data is to be stored.

Diskettes (floppy disks, 3.5-inch): Where information is stored; they can be transported and backed up. They should always be inserted into the disk drive with the top side (the side without the metal circle in the center) facing up. The edge of the rectangular metal bar should be inserted into the disk drive. If this is done properly, you will notice a small arrow indented into the plastic cover of the diskette. The arrow should point toward the Macintosh's disk drive.

Document: The file you create and modify with an application. A collection of information on a disk or in memory, grouped together and called by one name.

Double-clicking: Positioning the pointer and then quickly pressing and releasing the button on the mouse twice.

Dragging: Items on the computer screen can be moved about by dragging. Position the pointer on the icon or object and press the mouse button. While holding the mouse button down, move the pointer on the desktop surface. You'll see an outline of the object moving with the pointer, and when you release the mouse button, the object will move to the new location.

Enigma: The name for the underlying software technology that runs Finale.

ETF: Enigma Transportable File, a special file containing information that can be read across computer platforms, or even by a word processor.

Field: A box in a dialog box that you type information into, such as word or numerical data.

Finder: The program that generates the desktop and lets you locate and manage files and disks. Part of the Mac operating system.

Folder: A grouping of documents, applications, and other folders that is represented by a folder-shaped icon on the desktop. Equivalent to a sub-directory on the MS-DOS machines.

Font: A collection of letters, numbers, punctuation marks, and symbols with an identifiable and consistent look.

Handle: A small box that will appear in Finale scores, usually in the upper left-hand side of an entry. Can be used to resize, delete, and relocate entries.

Icon: A graphic representation of an object that looks like what it represents.

Interface: A device that allows for the transfer, input, or viewing of information. The computer screen is an interface that displays information. The way in which software is designed to accept data would be its interface.

Launch: Double-clicking on a computer application's icon to start or launch the program.

Library: Sets of musical symbols, expression markings, and other important musical elements that can be loaded into a document; the user can create or edit new symbols. Libraries can be opened or your personal library saved within the File option in the main Finale menu.

Macros: A combination of commands that may be called up by one computer command or keystroke(s).

Menu: A list of functions available in a computer program or part of a computer program.

Menu Bar: A bar used to select an option or command from a menu. May have pull-down options when a key word is selected with a mouse.

Metatools: These are available for many of the tools in Finale's Main Tool Palette. Metatools simplify notation input by programming the number keys 1 to 8 to a specific user-defined individual input option of a selected tool. Ex.: an individual articulation, key signature, time signature, dynamic, etc., can be programmed by simply holding down the Option key and selecting a numbered key (1-8). Once programmed, simply select a number and enter that tool option with the Enter key.

Mouse: A hand-held input device for a computer that rolls around on a trackball and contains one or more single click switch(es).

Noncontiguous: Items on a computer screen that are not next to each other. (See antonym, *Contiguous*)

Option Key: Helps to expand the scope of the alphanumeric keyboard to include additional characters and can have special functions with the different tools in Finale.

Page View: A navigational option in Finale where the music is laid out in sheet music form on the screen, one page at a time.

Pointer: What moves on the screen when you move the mouse. Its most common shapes are an arrow, I-beam, and wristwatch.

Pointing: By putting the tip of the pointer inside something on the desktop, window, or folder, you are pointing at it. If the pointer is not inside something, then you are not pointing at it.

RAM: Random Access Memory. A computer memory location that can be used over and over again to temporarily store data. Both computer applications and documents are placed into RAM as you work. You have to save your work from RAM to a floppy disk or hard drive, because all data in RAM is erased when you turn off your computer.

RAM is very important in that it allows computers to run an unlimited array of software.

Radio Button: ◉ A graphic image that is similar to the push buttons on older car radios; hence its name. When a radio button is selected to turn on a computer program option, another is deselected or pushed out; therefore, for each column in a dialog box containing radio buttons, only one button can be selected (as opposed to a box, where you may have multiple items selected).

Return Key: The Return key functions as a power key that will trigger the OK button in a dialog box or create a new paragraph in text input.

RTM: Read The Manual.

Scroll View: A navigation option in Finale where the music is viewed as a continuous horizontal band on the computer screen. The computer redraws the screen quickly in Scroll View.

Selection: Whatever is selected (highlighted, clicked on, etc.) will be affected by the next command or action.

Shift-clicking: Shift-clicking will allow you to select or deselect non-contiguous handles or objects. When you are inputting notes, holding down the Shift key will allow you to input rests.

Submenu: A main menu item may contain a submenu, showing other options which the user can select. You can tell if a menu item contains submenus by the inclusion of an arrow to the right of the command. To access the submenu options, drag the pointer to the right of the arrow and then release it on the submenu pop-up command list.

System: A musical term for a group of staves, each with individual clef-signs, designed to be read simultaneously rather than one by one.

Template: A Finale file that does not contain any note data but is pre-formatted for special layouts, such as grand staff for piano, tablature and staff guitar, etc. You can design your own or use the premade templates that come with Finale as a time saver when you create a score.

Toggle: A computer command option that allows you to move between two possible states, like a toggle switch. Ex: on or off, Page View or Scroll View, etc.

Window: In computer programs, a "screen-within-a screen" that is some subset of the main screen. A window may be opened or closed, and a window's contents are known collectively as the icon's *directory*.

Close Box—a small box in the upper-left corner of the window that will collapse the window.

Opening a Window—a window appears when an icon is opened in one of two ways: by going to the Open command in the File menu or by double-clicking on an icon.

Scroll Bar—A bar running along the left side and/or bottom of a window that allows you to move vertically or horizontally in a window to see more text or information.

Size Box—a box in the lower-right corner of the window that allows resizing of a window.

Title Bar—the top edge of a window.

Zoom Box—a box in the upper-right corner of a window. The two states for a window are small or filling the screen.

WYSIWYG: What You See Is What You Get. An image or score represented on your monitor that will look exactly the same when printed.

APPENDIX B

Step-by-Step Guide for Musical Score Creation

1. Whether you are working from an already existing musical score or a new score, number every measure lightly with a pencil (including repeats) as a reference.

2. Lay out your score in Finale—create the number of staves, measures, braces or brackets, staff names, and abbreviations that you will be using for the score's systems. You can also open a template (a time-saving pre-fabricated score layout without any notation). Select your measure numbering scheme.

3. Enter notes (Simple Entry and Speedy Entry).

4. Play back the score; check and correct wrong notes using the computer's built-in audio or MIDI.

5. Add articulations and expressions, either for individual staves or the entire score. You can specify that certain expressive markings that appear once in the score appear on all parts.

6. Play back the score; if you are using MIDI, added articulations and expressions will be aurally represented, allowing you to check proper or inappropriate placement in your score.

7. Add dynamics—these can either be added to one staff or the entire score.

8. Play back the score once again; if you are using MIDI, the added dynamics will be aurally represented; therefore, you can check proper or inappropriate placement in your score.

9. Add slurs and phrase marks.

10. Add lyrics; proceed very slowly and meticulously to avoid excessive mistakes and corrections. Finale contains a built-in text editor for lyrics, so all lyrics and text creation windows remain linked to the words on the page at all times. Changing lyrics in the text editor forces corresponding changes in the music.

11. Add word extensions (sustained-syllable underlines) to lyrics.

12. Add chord symbols. Finale will allow auto-assignment of chord symbols in either alphanumerical or fretboard notation. Finale can analyze chords from one or two staves and place them in your score. Configurable chord voicings also can play back on their own MIDI channel.

13. Adjust the size of the music with the Resize Tool for large scores.

14. (*Optional*) Optimize staff systems to remove resting instruments from the score.

15. Use the Apply Music Spacing and Update Layout commands.

16. Adjust the page turns; create measure groups if necessary. Add rehearsal marks.

17. Playback a final time for aural checking of accuracy, either from the built-in Macintosh speaker or a multitimbral MIDI synthesizer or sound module.

18. Prepare your manuscript for final printing output: add titles, text blocks, page numbers.

Creating a New Finale Default File

A Default Window is the first window that appears when you launch a program. Upon installation, a standard Finale Default File is placed in your computer's Finale Folder. This standard Finale Default File will display and contain the following: a single staff, one measure in the key of C, Metatool programming, staff and score expressions, font preferences, program options, and a common time signature. Many computer notation users specialize in working with a particular style or instrumental combination such as: piano, guitar, chamber ensemble, big band, orchestral, etc. If this case applies to you, it can be much more convenient to design an alternate default file. Keep in mind that you can only have one default file.

If you select Open from the File menu, you will see somewhere in the Finale folder a file called *Finale Default File* (see Figure AC-1).

If you create a new Finale document with all your preferences for working and replace the existing default window, this will now be the new default each time you launch Finale. To make a user-defined Finale Default File, follow these steps:

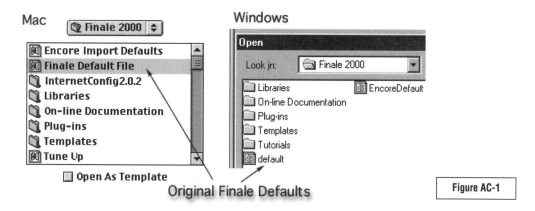

Figure AC-1

1. Create a Finale document without any notes (see Figure AC-2).

2. Custom program Metatools as you like to use them.

3. Select the measure numbering scheme you prefer.

Figure AC-2

4. Add fingerings or other often-used texts to the Staff or Score Expression Tool.

5. Select the music font you like to use (see Appendix 4).

6. Select your font preferences (see Appendix 4).

7. ▣ Mac   Save this file in your Finale folder with the exact title "Finale Default File."

   ▣ Windows   Save this file in your Finale folder with the exact title "DEFAULT.FTM"

It's that simple to create a new Finale Default File.

APPENDIX D

Using Special Notational Fonts

One of Finale's most powerful features is its ability to use different fonts (Petrucci is the font Finale normally uses) in a single document. Special music fonts can be purchased from Coda (Jazz—see Figure AD-1—or Golden Age handwritten style fonts) or Adobe (Sonata is an alternate traditional music font) and used to give your entire score or just a single element (lyrics, text, notation, or chords) a completely new appearance.

1. To use a special notational font, select the Options pull-down menu from the main menu and **Select Default Fonts** (see Figure AD-2).

Figure AD-1

2. The easiest way to change all the music is to select "Set Default Music Font" in the Select Default Fonts dialog box.

3. This will bring up a standard Select Font dialog box.

4. You can also select the font for lyrics (verse, chorus, section), chords (symbol, suffix, fretboard), notation (noteheads, accidentals, clefs, articulations, etc.), and text (repeats, measure numbers, staff names, etc.) in their dialog boxes.

5. After all the adjustments are selected, choose OK.

Figure AD-2

Lyrics: | Verse ▼ | Set Font... |

Times 10 plain

Exporting a Finale Selection to Text or Graphics Processors

Finale allows you to export single or multiple document pages or small portions of a page to a word processor or graphics program. This is a real asset for creating examples for a paper or textbook on music.

1. Have your music formatted with the Page Layout Tool as explained in Chapter Six; and choose Page View and then select the **Graphic Tool** 📇 .

2. Double-click and drag-enclose the page or page area that you want to export on the screen.

3. Go to the Graphics menu in the main menu and select the command **Export Selection.**

4. An Export Selection dialog box will appear:

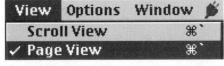

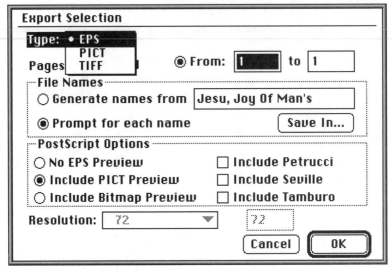

5. Select one of the three export options you can use from the Type menu: EPS, PICT, or TIFF.

6. Select where you will save the graphic with the [**Save In...**] button.

7. Choose a resolution setting in dots per inch if you are saving as a PICT or TIFF file. The higher the number, the greater the resolution or the more dots that will be available to represent your music.

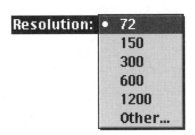

8. OK the Export Selection and Save dialog boxes. Open or Import into your graphic or word processor.

APPENDIX F

Swing Playback

Many jazz arrangers and educators use the less complicated notation of straight eighth notes with the expression *swing or swing feel* written in the score (see Figure AF-1). This is great for the performer or student reading a chart, but often it is helpful to have Finale play back the straight feel as swing rhythms. If this is the case and you wish to have nonswing notation play back with a swing feel, follow these steps.

Written Notation

Swing Playback

Figure AF-1

1. Select the **MIDI Tool** and click on the measure or measures that should play back with a swing feel.

2. Go to the MIDI menu at the top of the screen and select the command **Alter Feel** ... (see Figure AF-2).

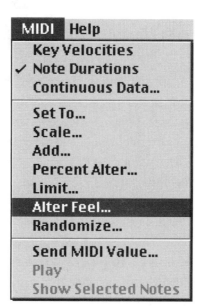

Figure AF-2

3. In the Alter Feel dialog box, type the number 171 in the Backbeats by field and select OK (see Figure AF-3). Play back your score, and it will now swing.

Figure AF-3

Alter Feel

Alter the Start and Stop Times of Any Notes that Begin or End on

Downbeats by 0

Other Beats by 0

Backbeats by 171   Cancel

● Absolute   OK
○ Percent of Original

APPENDIX G

Saving Scores As Standard MIDI Files

A Standard MIDI File (SMF) is a standardized way of transferring a Finale score to sequencing (Cakewalk, Vision, Performer), hard disk recording (Pro Tools), or multimedia software. There are three modes provided by this standard: 0 for a single multi-channel track (used by some dedicated sequencer playback units such as the Yamaha MFD-2), 1 for multiple MIDI channel tracks (most commonly used mode), and 2 for pattern-based multiple tracks. Check your software manual to find out which SMF it will open. This appendix provides a guide to help you successfully convert a Finale score to an SMF once note, chords, lyrics, expressions, etc. have been input.

As you add new staves to a Finale document, each additional one uses the same default MIDI channel and patch change unless you specify a different one. This creates a problem when creating a Standard MIDI File where independent MIDI channels become independent tracks when opened by sequencer, hard disk recording, or multimedia software. With Finale it is possible to assign each staff an independent MIDI channel number (1 through 16) and independent patch change number (1 through 128) using the Instrument Window in your main menu.

1. Open a new Finale document and create four different staves.

2. Select the **Instrument List** command from the Window menu, and the Instrument List dialog box will appear (see Figure AG-1).

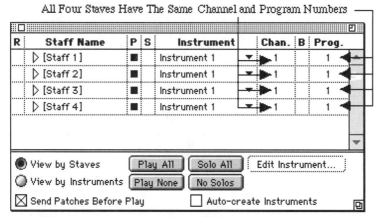

Figure AG-1

3. When you create a Staff Name it will be maintained with SMF transfer and used as the track name in the target software.

4. Select **New Instrument** from the Instrument List dialog box (see Figure AG-2).

Figure AG-2

5. The Instrument Definition dialog box will appear. Enter the following parameters as specified in Figure AG-3.

6. Create the following settings for the other three staves using the New Instrument pop-up menu and Instrument Definition dialog boxes. [Staff 2] Instrument Name: Bass, Channel: 2, Program Change: 33;

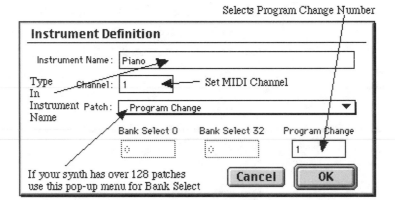

Selects Program Change Number

Instrument Definition

Instrument Name : | Piano |

Type
In   Channel: | 1 | — Set MIDI Channel

Instrument Patch: | Program Change ▼ |
Name

Bank Select 0   Bank Select 32   Program Change
| ○ | | ○ | | 1 |

If your synth has over 128 patches   [Cancel] [OK]
use this pop-up menu for Bank Select

Figure AG-3

[Staff 3] Instrument Name: Guitar, Channel: 3, Program Change: 25; [Staff 4] Instrument Name: Drums, Channel: 10, Program Change: 1. Now when you create an SMF from this document each instrument will be on its own track. If the default (all four staves on the same MIDI channel) was saved as an SMF, you would only have one track with all the instruments combined, not the desired result. Your Instrument List window should now look like Figure AG-4.

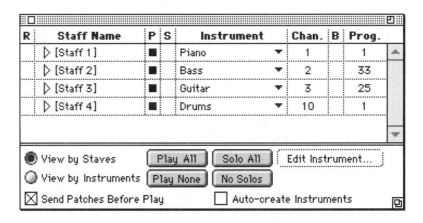

R	Staff Name	P	S	Instrument		Chan.	B	Prog.
	▷ [Staff 1]	■		Piano	▼	1		1
	▷ [Staff 2]	■		Bass	▼	2		33
	▷ [Staff 3]	■		Guitar	▼	3		25
	▷ [Staff 4]	■		Drums	▼	10		1

◉ View by Staves   [Play All] [Solo All]   [Edit Instrument...]
◯ View by Instruments   [Play None] [No Solos]
☒ Send Patches Before Play   ☐ Auto-create Instruments

Figure AG-4

7. The final step is to go to the File pull-down menu in the main menu and select Save As (Figure AG-5).

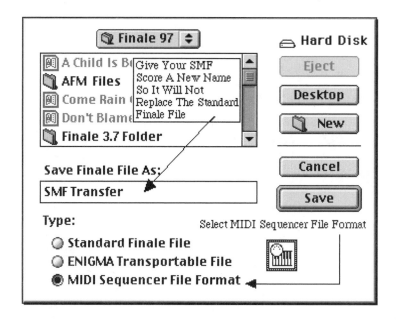

Figure AG-5

8. Notice how the icon in the lower right-hand corner has changed to represent an SMF 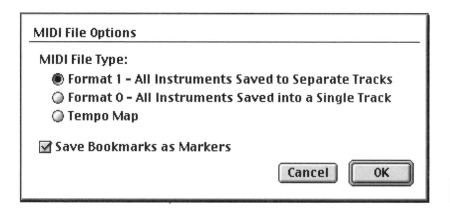.

9. Click on the Save button. A final dialog box will appear which asks to what SMF mode you want to save your file (Figure AG-6).

MIDI File Options

MIDI File Type:

● Format 1 – All Instruments Saved to Separate Tracks
○ Format 0 – All Instruments Saved into a Single Track
○ Tempo Map

☑ Save Bookmarks as Markers

Cancel   OK

Figure AG-6

10. Now you can open the SMF document in a sequencer or other type of application that can use SMF files. An SMF icon will represent SMF documents in your hard drive or storage medium, and a Standard Finale icon will represent Finale documents.

Windows to Mac Keyboard Shortcut Comparison Chart

Keyboard Shortcuts	Windows	Macintosh
File Menu		
New	*ctrl* - N	⌘- N
New (no default file)	Press *ctrl* when choosing New	Press *option* when choosing New
Open	*ctrl* - O	⌘ - O
Open (as "Untitled")	Press *ctrl* when choosing Open	Press *option* when choosing Open
Close	*ctrl* - W	⌘ - W
Save	*ctrl* - S	⌘ - S
Print Score	*ctrl* - P	⌘ - P
Quit / Exit (PC)	*alt* - F4	⌘ - Q
Edit Menu		
Undo	*ctrl* - Z	⌘ - Z
Cut	*ctrl* - X	⌘ - X
Copy	*ctrl* - C	⌘ - C
Select All	*ctrl* - A	⌘ - A
Update Layout	*ctrl* - U	⌘ - \
View Menu		
Page View	*ctrl* - E	⌘ - `
Scroll View	*ctrl* - E	⌘ - `
Home Position	Home key	⌘ - H
End Position	End key	*shift* - ⌘ - H

Keyboard Shortcuts	Windows	Macintosh
Redraw Screen	*ctrl* - D	⌘ - D
View at 200%	*ctrl* - F	⌘ - 2
View at 100%	*ctrl* - G	⌘ - 1
View at 75%	*ctrl* - J	⌘ - 7
View at 50%	*ctrl* - K	⌘ - 5
Define Staff Set	Press *ctrl* when choosing a Staff Set	*option* - *ctrl* - (1-8)

Hand Grabber Tool

Temporary Switch to Hand Grabber Tool	Press the *right* mouse button, and Drag	⌘ - *option* (and drag in score)

General Commands

Apply a Metatool	Press a number **(1-9)** and click the score	Press a number **(1-8)**
Program a Metatool	Press *ctrl* number **(1-9)**	Press *option* number **(1-8)**
Program keyboard equivalent for a tool	Press *shift* Function key **(F2-F12)**	*option* - *ctrl* - **(1-8)**
Switch to a tool you've programmed	Press Function key **(F2-F12)**	*option* - *ctrl* - **(1-8)**

Window Menu

Show / hide Main Tool Palette	Not available	⌃⌘ - T

Playback

Begin / Pause playing	Space bar	Space bar
"Scrub" onscreen music	*ctrl* - space bar (and drag in the score)	*option* - space bar (and drag in the score)

Simple Entry

Whole note—128th note	Press a key **(0-8)** and click the staff	Press a key **(0-8)** and click the staff
Whole rest—128th note	Press *shift* and a key **(0-8)**; click the staff	Press *shift* and a key **(0-8)**; click the staff

Keyboard Shortcuts   Windows   Macintosh

Speedy Entry

	Windows	Macintosh
Remove note, rest, or chord	(delete)	(delete)
Hide / show note or rest	Letter **O**	Letter **O**
Add or remove accidental parentheses	Letter **P**	Letter **P**
Jump to previous measure	[	[
Jump to next measure	]	]
Flip stem in opposite direction	Letter **L**	Letter **L**
Restore stem direction to "floating" status	(ctrl) - **L**	(option) - **L**
Change to / from grace note	;	;
Voice 1/2	' (apostrophe)	' (apostrophe)
Cycle through layers 1 to 4	(shift) - ' (apostrophe)	(shift) - (↑) upward 4 to 1 (shift) - (↓) downward 1 to 4
Move editing frame down a staff	(shift) - (↓)	(return)
Move editing frame up a staff	(shift) - (↑)	(shift) - (return)
Constrain dragging a note (horizontal / vertical)	(shift) - drag	(shift) - drag
Define a tuplet	(ctrl) - **1**	(option) - **(2-8)**
Raise by a half step	**+** (plus)	**+** (plus)
Lower by a half step	**−** (minus)	**−** (minus)
Raise by a half step (for entire measure)	(ctrl) - **+** (plus)	(option) - **+** (plus)
Lower by a half step (for entire measure)	(ctrl) - **−** (minus)	(option) - **−** (minus)
Previous note	(←)	(←)
Next note	(→)	(→)

Keyboard Shortcuts   Windows   Macintosh

Speedy Entry

	Windows	Macintosh
Down a step	↓	↓
Up a step	↑	↑
Remove note from chord	delete	clear
Change a single note to a rest	delete	clear
Tie / untie to next note	=	=
Break / join beam from previous note	/	/
Show / hide courtesy accidental	*	*
Restore courtesy accidental to optional status	ctrl - *	option - *
Exit measure and redraw / re-enter measure	**0** - zero	**0** - zero
Flip a note to its enharmonic equivalent	**9**	**9**
Flip enharmonic throughout measure	ctrl - **9**	option - **9**
Add a dot	. (period)	. (period)
Add a note to a chord	enter	enter
Change a rest to a note	enter	enter
Specify a pitch, high C–B (without MIDI)	**Q - W - E - R - T - Y - U**	**Q - W - E - R - T - Y - U**
Specify a pitch, middle C–B (without MIDI)	**A - S - D - F - G - H - J**	**A - S - D - F - G - H - J**
Specify a pitch, low C–B (without MIDI)	**Z - X - C - V - B - N - M**	**Z - X - C - V - B - N - M**
Raise all pitch keys an octave	**, (comma)**	**, (comma)**
Lower all pitch keys an octave	**I**	**I**
Restore all pitch keys to normal register	**K**	**K**

Zoom Tool

	Windows	Macintosh
Zoom in (enlarge 2x, if tool is selected)	click the score	click the score
Zoom out (reduce by 1/2, if tool is selected)	ctrl - click the score	option - click the score

Conventional Instrument Transposition Chart

Inst. Family	Inst. Name	Key of Inst.	Transposition	
WOODWIND (G) Up P4	Alto Flute	In G	Written / Sounding	1st
(F) Up P5	English Horn		Written / Sounding	2nd
(Bb) up Maj 2	Clarinet	In Bb	Written / Sounding	3rd
(A) up mi3	Clarinet	In A	Written / Sounding	4th
(Bb treble clef) Up Maj 9	Bass Clarinet	In Bb	Written / Sounding French System	5th
(Bb) up Maj 2	Sop. Sax	In Bb	Written / Sounding	6th
(Eb) Up Maj6	Alto Sax	In Eb	Written / Sounding	7th
(Bb treble clef) Up Maj 9	Tenor Sax	In Bb	Written / Sounding	8th

Inst. Family	Inst. Name	Key of Inst.	Transposition		
(Eb treble clef) Up Maj6 + Octave	Baritone Sax	In Eb	Written — Sounding		9th
	Bass Sax	In Bb	Written — Sounding		10th
BRASS	Trombone Baritone Tuba	No Transposition			
(F) Up P5	Horns	In F	Written — Sounding		11th
(Bb) up Maj 2	Trumpets	In Bb	Written — Sounding		12th
(Bb) up Maj 2	Cornets	In Bb	Written — Sounding		13th

Finale is designed to display instrumental parts either at concert pitch (which can be printed to create a concert score) or at transposition for the performer or conductor. If MIDI playback is desired, the CMN software must convert transposed instruments to concert pitch (for playback with nontransposing instruments without problems).

Score Order

Each family of instruments should be grouped together in a score with the highest to lowest pitched instruments from the top to the bottom of the group. The exception to this rule is the French Horn, which is at the top of brass, although it is not the highest in pitch.

Quartets

String	Woodwind
Violin I	Flute
Violin II	Oboe
Viola	Clarinet
Violoncello or Cello	Bassoon

Quintets

Woodwind	Brass
Flute	Trumpet I
Oboe	Trumpet II
Clarinet	French Horn
French Horn	Trombone
Bassoon	Tuba

Sextets & Stage or Jazz Band

Brass	Jazz Band (Stage Band)
Trumpet I	Saxophones
Trumpet II	Trumpets
French Horn	Trombones
Trombone	Guitar

Euphonium (Baritone)	Upright or Electric Bass
Tuba	Drums
Piano	Piano

Orchestra & Concert Band

Orchestra	Concert Band
Flutes	Flutes
Oboes	Oboes
Bassoons	Bassoons
Clarinets	Clarinets
Saxophones	*Saxophones*
Bassoons	Bassoons
Saxophones	*Saxophones*
French Horns	French Horns
Trumpets	Trumpets
Trombones	Trombones
Tuba	Euphonium (Baritone)
Timpani	Tuba
Percussion	Timpani
Other Instruments – *saxophones, harp, piano, celesta, organ, voices, chorus, solo instruments*	Percussion
Violin I	
Violin II	
Viola	
Violoncello or cello	
Contrabass	

Bibliography
For Further Study

Additional Books on Finale

Metzger, David. *Finale and Jazz Arranging*
  • David Metzger Music 3545 Hulsey Avenue,
  SE, Salem, Oregon 97302 (503) 371-400,
  105 pages, 1993.

Books on Music Notation

Cole, Hugo. *Sounds and Signs: Aspects of Musical
  Notation* • Oxford University Press, London,
  300 pages, 1974.

Gerou, Tom & Lusk, Linda. *Essential Dictionary of
  Musical Notation (the most practical and concise
  source for music notation)* • (ISBN 0-88284-
  730-9), Alfred Publishing Co. Inc., Los Ange-
  les, 352 pages, 1996.

Harder, Paul O. *Music Manuscript Techniques
  (A Programmed Approach)* • (ISBN 0-205-
  07992-X [Pt. 1], 0-205-07993-8 [Pt. 2]),
  Crescendo Publishers, Boston, 482 pages,
  1984.

Read, Gardner. *Music Notation (A Manual of Modern Practice)* • (ISBN 0-8008-5453-5), Allyn
  and Bacon Inc., Boston, 300 pages, 1979.

Rosenthal, Carl A. *Practical Guide to Music Notation for Composers, Arrangers, and Editors.*
  • MCA Music, New York, 345 pages, 1967.

Ross, Ted. *Teach Yourself the Art of Music Engraving*
  • Hansen House, Miami Beach, FL, 278
  pages, 1987.

Stone, Kurt. *Music Notation in the Twentieth Century (A Practical Guidebook)* • W. W. Norton
  & Company, New York, 335 pages, 1980.

Articles on Music Notation

Stone, Kurt. "New Music Notation—Why?"
  • *Musical America (in High Fidelity)*, XXIV/7
  (July 1974, pp. 16-20.

Stone, Kurt. "New Notation for New Music
  (Parts I and II)", *Music Educators Journal*
  • LX-III/2 (October 1976), pp. 48-56, and
  LXIII/3 (November 1976) pp. 14-28.

Books on Computers
and Music Education

Mash, David. *Computers and the Music Educator*
  • (Phone 800/963-TREE), SoundTree
  Publishing Co., New York, 102 pages, 1996.

Music Educators National Conference. *The School
  Music Program: A New Vision* • (ISBN 1-
  56545-039-6), MENC, Reston VA, 1-800-336-
  3768, 42 pages, 1994.

Rudolph, E. Thomas. *Teaching Music with Technology* • (ISBN 094105092-0), GIA
  Publications, Inc., Chicago, 316 pages, 1996.

Electronic Music & Music References

Anderton, Craig. *The Electronic Musician's Dictionary* • (ISBN 0-8256-1125-3), Amsco Publications, New York, NY, 119 pages, 1988.

Apel, Willie. *Harvard Dictionary of Music*
  • (ISBN 0-674-37501-7), Belknap Press of
  Harvard University Press, Cambridge, MA,
  935 pages, 1981.

Lee, William. *Music in the 21st Century: The New
  Language* • (ISBN 0-7604-0065-2), CPP/Bel-
  win, Inc., Miami Florida, 193 pages, 1994.

Tomlyn, Bo & Leonard, Steve. *Electronic Music
  Dictionary: A glossary of specialized terms relat-
  ing to the music and sound technology of today*
  • (ISBN 0-88188-904-0), Hal Leonard
  Books, Milwaukee, WI, 77 pages, 1988.

Index